Notes on the Church Year for Children

Take Me Home

BY CHRISTINE KENNY-SHEPUTIS

I prefer to cut
children's spiritual garments
a little large,
for them to grow into,
as they will in time.
And who knows
what vivid image or hint
of the beauty of God
may remain in their mind
and memory?

Dorothy Coddington
Orate Fratres, **1949**

Prayer for Martin Luther King's Birthday © The Liturgical Conference, Washington DC. Used with permission

Prayer for Labor Day is an excerpt from the *Book of Common Prayer,* © Church Pension Fund. Used with permission.

LITURGY TRAINING PUBLICATIONS

TAKE ME HOME: NOTES ON THE CHURCH YEAR FOR CHILDREN © 1991 Archdiocese of Chicago: Liturgy Training Publications, 1800 North Hermitage Avenue, Chicago, Illinois 60622-1101; 1-800-933-1800; orders@ltp.org; fax 1-800-933-7094; www.ltp.org.

This book was illustrated by Suzanne Novak and designed by Mary Bowers. Editing was done by Peter Mazar, with editorial assistance by Theresa Pincich and Lorraine Schmidt. Typesetting was done by James Mellody-Pizzato. The principal typeface is 13 point Sabon; headlines are set in Univers.

04 03 02 01 00   7 6 5 4 3

ISBN 0-929650-52-2

INTRODUCTION

The 60 notes in this book are meant to be photocopied and handed out to students and then to be taken home. The book offers something for each week of the year. The purchase of this book gives you permission to duplicate these notes for a parish or school.

Take Me Home *notes can be hung on the refrigerator at home and can be read and used during the week.* Nevada artist Suzanne Novak has included simple and beautiful illustrations that can be colored by children. These notes can serve as a reminder of a special day or season coming up. They can help join the liturgical life of the parish with our kitchens and living rooms and gardens.

The sacramental life of the church uses the materials of this world as signs of the world to come, signs of God's kingdom that we await and that, in mystery, is already here among us. The church uses water and oil, bread and wine, gestures, processions, singing, proclamations and even special clothing in the liturgy at the various forms of public, communal prayer that mark Lord's Days, or mornings and evenings, or when new members are baptized or two people are wed or the dead are buried.

There is also the sacramental life of the domestic church. The church celebrates at home with all kinds of materials and methods. Some of the most profound prayers of Christians may have the spicy aroma of a Pentecost barbecue or the taste of a Transfiguration Day picnic. A November visit to a graveyard or an Advent visit to a tree lot can be a glimpse into heaven, a touching of eternity. And these wonders are the common property of Christians six or sixty years old, single or married, alone or in the company of others.

Here in this book you will find suggestions for praying by snipping evergreens or mixing cookie dough or hiding hard-boiled eggs in the backyard. Here are ideas for prayer offered while fixing supper or taking a shower or riding a bus. This is hands-on "holy play." And it is the kind of play best accomplished when all kinds of folks play together.

The language of these take-home notes is straightforward; the project was given to fourth graders to read and comment on. Here and there, teachers and parents may need to help children with the vocabulary, and that's how any learning material should be. It was not imagined that children can make full use of *Take Me Home* without cooperation from the members of their households. What is hoped is that everyone using these notes gets caught up in learning, experimentation, discovery.

These notes will enter the home as something of a challenge: Children will be bringing into the house a piece of paper that sometimes speaks about ovens, candles, scissors, and occasionally even the spending of money. This can be dangerous information. It also can be a nuisance because the notes ask parents to play an active part in the liturgical life of the home.

But not every person has a prayer life. Not every child has parents or even a home. Parents and children already may be taxed for time, for interest, for resources. These notes may not be welcome without a religious educator's groundwork and advice and sensitive guidance.

Assure students and their families that these notes are not some form of required homework. They are, instead, springboards for family discussion, often just something to think about. Maybe every so often one of these notes will be the right thing at the right time, but not always. Urge adaptation, suggest alternatives and remain attuned to the special needs of individuals in your care.

We have tried to be practical. Illinois author Christine Kenny-Sheputis has "kitchen tested" these ideas in her household. She has drawn from a wide range of Christian traditions. So the ideas have been "time-tested," too. Ms. Kenny-Sheputis has not collected gimmicks here. What she has put together are worthy customs in celebration of the gospel.

All in all, a rich array of traditions is represented (although, of course, there is much that is not here—a limitation of any printed resource). We have tried to include as many ethnic groups as we could, giving an emphasis to customs that transcend national divisions. Many saints' days are included. Most of the church feast days are presented here. Because of the importance of these seasons, each week of Lent and Eastertime has its own page.

Some of the notes are for the same day every year, like St. Lucy's Day on December 13. Some of the notes cannot be dated in this book because they deal with "movable feasts," such as Easter and the many days that depend on the date of Easter.

In this book, for some weeks there are two or more choices of handouts to be sent home. For instance, perhaps one year you might send home the entry for Our Lady of Guadalupe (December 12) and the next year you might send home the one about St. Lucy—or you can send home both. You will want to think ahead to send home notes early enough so they can be used to plan coming days and seasons.

On the facing page of each note are a few suggestions for use and perhaps a brief synopsis of a season. We also have suggested the color of the paper that these notes might best be printed on. You might find it easiest to photocopy several weeks' worth of notes at one time. Different colored papers will help you distinguish the notes—and will make them more lively, too.

CONTENTS

5TH WEEK OF EASTER
Our Easter Zoo

6TH WEEK OF EASTER
Firstfruits of Easter

7TH WEEK OF EASTER
Unbabbling Babel

PENTECOST
A Fiery Finale

TRINITY SUNDAY
Keeping Holy the Lord's Day

BODY & BLOOD OF CHRIST
Planting Paradise

2ND SUNDAY IN MAY
Mother's Day ▪ Honor Your Many Mothers

3RD SUNDAY IN JUNE
Father's Day ▪ Tell Me a Story

JUNE 24
Birth of John the Baptist ▪
The Midsummer Nativity

JUNE 29
Apostles Peter and Paul ▪
Give Us This Day Our Daily Bread

JULY 4
Independence Day ▪
A Day to Make Memories

JULY 14
Martyr Kateri Tekakwitha ▪
The Lily of the Mohawks

JULY 22, 25 AND 29
Mary Magdalene, James and Martha ▪
Patrons of Summertime Hospitality

AUGUST 6
Transfiguration of the Lord ▪
Climbing God's Holy Mountain

AUGUST 15
Assumption of Mary ▪
Our Lady of the Harvest

AUGUST 24
Apostle Bartholomew ▪ St. Bart's Day

1ST MONDAY IN SEPT.
Labor Day ▪ A Labor of Love

SEPTEMBER 4
Moses the Lawgiver ▪ Mind Your Mannas

SEPTEMBER 8
Birth of Mary ▪ What's in a Name?

SEPTEMBER 14
Triumph of the Cross ▪
We Should Glory in the Cross

SEPTEMBER 21
Apostle Matthew ▪ Patron of the Unpopular

SEPTEMBER 27
Vincent de Paul ▪ Monsieur Vincent

SEPTEMBER 29
*Archangels Michael, Gabriel
and Raphael* ▪ Michaelmas

OCTOBER 4
Francis of Assisi ▪ A Simple Saint

SUKKOT
*the Jewish Festival
of Harvest Homes* ▪
Shine on, Harvest Moon!

OCTOBER 18
Evangelist Luke ▪ Luke, the Ox

OCTOBER 31
Halloween ▪ All Hallows

NOVEMBER 1
All Saints' Day ▪
When All the Saints Go Marchin' In . . .

NOVEMBER 2
All Souls' Day ▪ A-Souling We Will Go!

NOVEMBER 11
Bishop Martin of Tours ▪ Martinmas

SUNDAY BEFORE ADVENT
Christ the King ▪ A Crown for King Jesus

4TH THURSDAY IN NOV.
Thanksgiving ▪ We Gather Together

First Sunday of Advent

The season of Advent lasts from the evening before the fourth Sunday before Christmas until Christmas Eve. Advent is a season of hope, expectancy and eager anticipation. Advent is a rehearsal for what all our days must be, "as we wait in joyful hope for the coming of our Savior, Jesus Christ."

Religious educators have a special responsibility to foster Advent's spirit of waiting and patience and vigilance. Teachers have a unique charge to build up an appreciation for the spirit of the liturgy and for the church's calendar, especially when that calendar is in contrast to commercial propaganda that ignores Advent and that rushes us too soon into Christmas.

The take-home notes in this book for Advent would be particularly attractive photocopied on buff, purple, gray, rose or blue paper. You might distribute this first note for Advent along with the words of an Advent song to sing at home.

ADVENT

Wait for the Lord

Everything is building toward Christmas, but our season now is Advent, not Christmas.

Advent is the time before December 25. Christmas begins on Christmas Day and lasts until well into the new year. Advent is a time to wait for Christmas, and there are many ways for us to wait.

Wait until as close as possible to Christmas Day before decorating your home. That way you won't be bored with the decorations by the time Christmas finally comes. During Advent you can get the decorations ready. Maybe you can make decorations for others to surprise them at Christmas.

Plan to turn your Christmas lights on and to light your tree for the first time on Christmas Eve. That way, you will create a great burst of light all at once to welcome Christ. During Advent, you will want to get those lights ready and make sure they work.

During Advent, the days keep growing shorter. The night sky in winter is very beautiful. In Advent, you can celebrate the darkness by turning off extra lights to save electricity. You can take an evening walk to look at the stars. If you are afraid of the dark, remember that when Christmas comes, the days will start growing longer again.

Advent is a time to plan and prepare. Plan now to keep the days after Christmas Day with gift and cookie exchanges, caroling parties, puppet shows, pageants and winter carnivals. Who will you invite to make merry with you this Christmastime?

Copyright © 1991, Liturgy Training Publications, 1-800-933-1800. Written by Christine Kenny-Sheputis. Art by Suzanne Novak.

Memorial of St. Nicholas +c350, bishop
December 6

The Wonder-Worker

Copyright © 1991, Liturgy Training Publications, 1-800-933-1800. Written by Christine Kenny-Sheputis. Art by Suzanne Novak.

Nicholas was bishop of the city of Myra, in what now is the country of Turkey. He was known for his charity. He welcomed homeless people to live in his home. Once he even turned his home into a hospital.

Nicholas is called a "wonder-worker" because he performed many miracles. His greatest miracle was the example of his own life. Many people saw the good things Nicholas did and were inspired to do good things, too.

On St. Nicholas's Day, December 6, the bishop's fans rush to follow his wonderful example of giving gifts to people in secret.

One custom is for people to leave out their shoes or to hang stockings on the night before St. Nicholas's Day. These are filled—by you or by anyone in the house—in imitation of the saint. Popular fillers are small tangerines, nuts, gold foil-wrapped chocolates and, especially, gingerbread cookies. These can be tokens of love, beautifully shaped and iced, perhaps wrapped in tissue, and set beside each shoe or handed out at school.

Make a gingerbread cookie recipe. Roll out and cut the dough into shapes of boys, girls, St. Nicholas or hearts. Then whip 1⅓ cups of powdered sugar with 1 egg white and a pinch of cream of tartar. Spoon the icing into a plastic sandwich bag and squeeze it into a corner. Twist the excess plastic to seal the opening and snip the tiniest bit of the filled corner so you can squeeze out the icing in a thin line. Decorate your cookies beautifully.

TAKE ME HOME

Feast of Our Lady of Guadalupe
December 12

Copyright © 1991, Liturgy Training Publications, 1-800-933-1800. Written by Christine Kenny-Sheputis. Art by Suzanne Novak.

Nuestra Señora de Guadalupe

The feast of Our Lady of Guadalupe is a remembrance of the day in 1531 when Mary appeared in Mexico to Juan Diego. She left a picture of herself on his cloak. In this picture, she is an Indian, like Juan Diego, and she shines with the light of the sun, moon and stars. Mary is wrapped in a *cinto,* the sash that was worn by women when they were pregnant. Our Lady of Guadalupe is pregnant with Christ.

This Advent feast calls many Mexican people from their homes before dawn. At about 4:00 AM, in the deep darkness of December, people gather outside churches to offer up their morning serenade *(mañanitas)* to Mary. In time, the church doors swing open and everyone celebrates Mass.

Afterward, there's a grand breakfast—pastries, sweet Mexican chocolate, hot bread and *menudo,* which is a hot tripe soup rich with garlic, thickened with hominy and sparked with the sting of *ancho* and *pasilla* peppers. *Menudo* is garnished with diced radishes, fresh cilantro, oregano, lime juice and chopped onion. It's quite a breakfast!

Our Lady of Guadalupe is the patron of all the peoples of the Western Hemisphere. Celebrate the feast by learning about the cultures of Mexico. Wake up extra early that day and offer your Advent morning song to Mary. And toast her with a cup of cocoa.

Memorial of St. Lucy +304, virgin martyr
December 13

Lucy Cats

Copyright © 1991, Liturgy Training Publications, 1-800-933-1800. Written by Christine Kenny-Sheputis. Art by Suzanne Novak.

Lucy was a young girl who was martyred in Sicily in the year 304. Lucy's name means "light." Lucy supposedly owned a pet cat. Cats can see at night. Their eyes reflect even weak light. So cats' eyes seem to glow, as if they have a bit of Lucy's own light inside of them.

Follow a Swedish tradition and bake *Leissi Kattor*, "St. Lucy's cats," for her day, December 13. You will need 1 pound of frozen bread dough, at least 24 dried currants or raisins, an egg, a ribbon, a cookie sheet and clean scissors.

Start two days before. Follow the directions on the package to thaw the frozen bread dough.

When you are ready to bake, divide the thawed dough into 12 equal parts. Take a gum-ball-size piece of dough from each of the 12 parts. Roll it between your hands into a tail for each cat. Set aside. Form each piece of dough into a smooth oval. Squeeze the dough to make it look like a head at one end and twist the head once to make a neck. Attach the tail at the other end and curve it around the body.

Make two scissor snips in the top of each head; pinch little ears from them. Snip slits for eyes and press currants or raisins into them. Place cats on a cookie sheet, about 1½ inches apart. Brush each with beaten egg and set aside for 1 hour to rise in a warm place. Preheat the oven to 350°.

Bake cats 30 minutes until golden. When cooled, tie a ribbon around each of their necks.

The O Antiphons

During the final week of Advent, the church
begins to proclaim the gospels from Matthew and
Luke about the annunciations and births of John
the Baptist and Jesus. Advent's spirit of expec-
tation reaches a crescendo. This spirit is expressed
in the seven O Antiphons, so named because
each begins with the word "O."

The O Antiphons are chanted from December
17 to 23 at evening Prayer as a refrain to the
Magnificat, Mary's song of praise. The antiphons
also are prayed at the eucharist as part of the
gospel acclamation. The antiphons have been
set metrically in the popular hymn "O come,
O come, Emmanuel."

Perhaps the hymn can be copied along with this
take-home note for distribution.

O Come, O Come, Emmanuel!

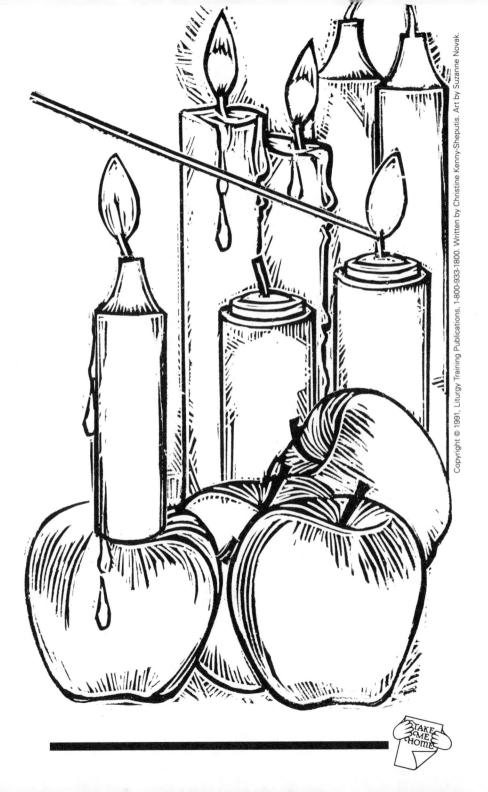

Copyright © 1991, Liturgy Training Publications, 1-800-933-1800. Written by Christine Kenny-Sheputis. Art by Suzanne Novak.

During the final week of Advent, we become very eager for Christmas and for Christ to come. The whole church becomes eager.

We say special prayers for each day of the final week of Advent. In the prayers, we ask Jesus to come soon. Beginning on December 17, at sunset, an "O Antiphon" is sung. For seven days, a different O Antiphon is sung each evening. The O Antiphons begin with titles for Jesus. The titles were chosen from the Bible.

If you know the song "O come, O come, Emmanuel," you know a version of the O Antiphons! Find a hymnal and sing the correct verse each evening:

December 17's begins "O Wisdom." December 18's is "O Adonai," which means "Lord" in the Hebrew language. December 19's is "O Flower of Jesse." (Jesse was King David's father.) December 20's is "O Key of David." Why do you think Jesus is called these strange and marvelous names?

The antiphon for December 21's—the shortest day of the year, when winter begins—is "O Daystar" (a wonderful old word for the sun). December 22's is "O King." December 23's is "O Emmanuel," which means "God is with us."

On December 24 at sundown, Christmas Eve, our Advent waiting is over and Christmas begins!

Christmas Day
December 25

Twelve Days of Christmas
December 26 to January 6

Christmastime lasts from the evening before Christmas Day until the feast of the Baptism of the Lord (usually the second Sunday in January). Considering the cultural pressure to end Christmas once gifts are unwrapped, it is especially important for religious educators to do what they can to make the church's celebration of Christmastime popular and appealing.

The English call the twelve days *after* December 25 "The Twelve Days of Christmas" (as in the familiar carol). The Germans and other central Europeans begin their count on Christmas Day; they consider January 6 the "thirteenth day." Either way, there are a baker's dozen of days in which we end one year and begin a new in celebration of Christ, the Lord of time and history.

The take-home notes for Christmastime would be attractive on gold or green paper. (Notes duplicated on red paper can be difficult to read.)

In These Twelve Days Let Us Be Glad!

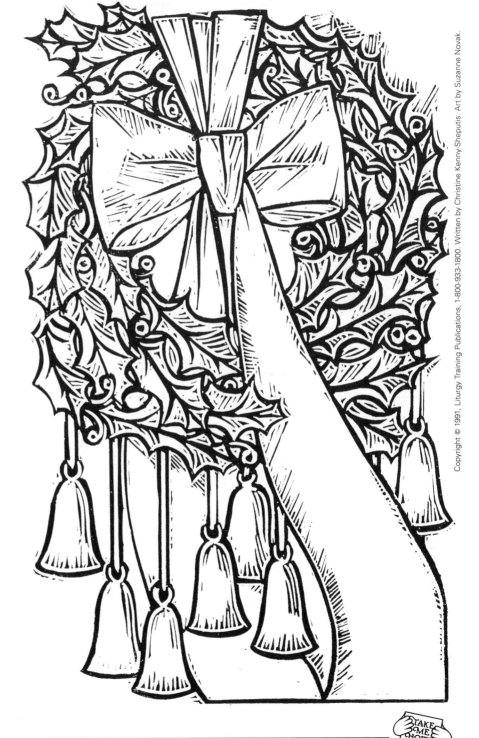

Did you know that the "Twelve Days of Christmas" come *after* Christmas Day? They run from December 26 to January 6. Together with December 25, they make 13, a "baker's dozen" of days. Here are a few ideas for a merrier Christmastime:

Each night from Christmas Day until Epiphany, move the statues of the Magi bit by bit closer to your nativity scene. They can travel through the house, maybe visiting each room. On Epiphany, they arrive at Bethlehem.

If there will be several gifts for each person, try spacing them out over the Twelve Days. Open one each night. That way, the surprises will keep on coming.

St. Stephen's Day, December 26, is a perfect night to go caroling. "Good King Wenceslas" is about a saint who fed a poor man on "the feast of Stephen." The carol is fun to sing as a round—like "Row, row, row your boat." The day after caroling, take a gift to a food pantry.

On Holy Innocents' Day, December 28, honor the children who died when King Herod tried to kill Jesus. This is the church's "Children's Day," called *Childermas.* One family keeps their Christmas lights dark and tries not to eat any Christmas treats this day to remember all innocent people who have been killed.

On New Year's Eve, chase away the old year by blowing horns and clanging bells. See if you can invite guests for dinner tomorrow. A guest in the home is Christ in the home. Be sure to invite Christ to keep Christmastime with you!

Copyright © 1991, Liturgy Training Publications, 1-800-933-1800. Written by Christine Kenny-Sheputis. Art by Suzanne Novak.

TAKE ME HOME

Solemnity of the Epiphany of the Lord

Epiphany is not the end of Christmas. It is the high point of Christmas. (Christmastime ends on the feast of the Baptism of the Lord, and it echoes until February 2, Candlemas.)

In many ways, Epiphany is the grandest, most exuberant, most giddy feast on the church's calendar. The Epiphany liturgy—the scriptures, prayer texts, chants and blessings—just about explodes with superlatives. It is a wonderful challenge for religious educators to share this exuberance with the parish at home, at worship and in class.

Among Roman Catholics in the United States and Canada, Epiphany is celebrated on the first Sunday after January 1. It is celebrated on January 6, its ancient day, by many other Christians in North America and throughout the rest of the world. You might want to distribute this take-home note during the week of January 1 or before Christmas vacation.

Arise and Shine!

On Epiphany, Christ is revealed to the world. The Magi offer gifts to their newborn King. The River Jordan leaps up to baptize Jesus. Water becomes wine at Cana. The star of Bethlehem drives away the darkness of night to welcome the Messiah, the Prince of Peace.

Epiphany is the merriest day of Christmastime. We can make our homes and neighborhoods glitter with gold and fragrantly smell from frankincense and myrrh. A big part of the Epiphany celebration is the blessing of the home in the new year.

On a night when members of the household sit down to supper together, before dinner, divide a cake into as many pieces as you have people. Hide a dried bean or coin in one of them. At dessert, pass the pieces around. Whoever finds the bean becomes the queen or king for the night and gets to lead the blessing. Give the royal person a crown to wear, a piece of chalk and an evergreen sprig with a bowl of water.

Gather at the front door and pray the Our Father. The crowned person writes in chalk over the door:

$$20 + C + M + B + 0X$$

The numbers should be those of the new year. The crosses stand for the four seasons. The letters stand for the names of the three Magi: Caspar, Melchior and Balthasar.

Now move through the rooms of the house, and sprinkle them with water, and sing "We three kings" and "Joy to the world" to bring Christ's blessing to your home in this glad new year of grace.

TAKE ME HOME

Copyright © 1991, Liturgy Training Publications, 1-800-933-1800. Written by Christine Kenny-Sheputis. Art by Suzanne Novak.

Feast of the Baptism of the Lord

Feast of the Baptism of the Lord

Beloved Children of God

At Jesus' birth, Mary showed Jesus to the world as her son. At Jesus' baptism, God the Father showed Jesus as the Son of God. At our own baptism, we claimed God as a parent. And God claimed us as beloved children. If you can get there, visit the place where you were baptized. Look at a baptismal font. Remember other baptisms you've seen.

The new year is an important time for visiting relatives and friends. These are good days to recall your entry into the family of God by paying your godparents a special visit.

In one part of England, triangular "godcakes"—for the Holy Trinity—were exchanged at the new year. You can use three-cornered apple or cherry turnovers for god-cakes. Or, with an adult's help, you can make your own with store-bought pie dough.

Roll and cut the dough into 3-inch squares. Put a teaspoon of mincemeat or any pie filling in the center of each square. Fold them into triangles and crimp the edges with a fork. Bake at 425° until golden. When cooled, dust them with powdered sugar.

When Jesus was baptized, the sky opened up, and the Holy Spirit appeared like a dove. Celebrate the baptism of Jesus by hanging a Christmas dove over the supper table. Have your godparents over for dinner and serve them godcakes for dessert. Everyone can join in the carol "Joy to the world." On this day "heaven and nature sing" that Jesus Christ is Lord—including skies and rivers and doves, and you, too!

TAKE ME HOME

Dr. Martin Luther King, Jr., Day
Third Monday in January

MARTIN LUTHER KING

Mine Eyes Have Seen the Glory . . .

Celebrate the memory and the work of Martin Luther King, Jr., today!

Dr. King led many people in the country—and in the world, too—to work hard for fairness among people of different races and religions. He taught that the best way to make the world a better place was through nonviolent methods. Thinking up nonviolent ways to make good changes in our society is hard work.

Dr. King was born on January 15, 1929. On April 6, 1968, Dr. King was murdered for what he taught and did. Here is a special prayer for this national holiday from the book *Catholic Household Blessings and Prayers*:

Lord our God,
see how oppression and violence are
    our sad inheritance,
one generation to the next.

We look for you where the lowly are raised up,
where the mighty are brought down.
We find you there in your servants,
and we give you thanks this day
for your preacher and witness,
    Martin Luther King, Jr.

Fill us with your spirit:
where our human community is divided by racism,
torn by repression, saddened by fear and ignorance,
and may we give ourselves to your work of healing.

Grant this through Christ our Lord. Amen.

TAKE ME HOME

Copyright © 1991, Liturgy Training Publications, 1-800-933-1800. Written by Christine Kenny-Sheputis. Art by Suzanne Novak.

Memorial of St. Anthony +325, abbot
January 17

The Patron of Pets

Copyright © 1991, Liturgy Training Publications, 1-800-933-1800. Written by Christine Kenny-Sheputis. Art by Suzanne Novak.

St. Anthony lived in Egypt as a hermit. A hermit is a person who lives alone to pay close attention to prayer. But, according to legend, Anthony did not quite live alone. He had lots of pets—chickens, goats, donkeys, cats, dogs, birds and fish.

Eventually, Anthony called together other hermits into a community. They found they could pray well and live together as Christians. Anthony became the community's abbot, a word meaning "father." He was called their father because everyone lived together like a family.

When he fasted, Anthony lived on bread and water. According to another legend about the saint, Satan entered a pig and began to tempt Anthony. Maybe the devil thought Anthony wanted a dinner of roast pork. But Anthony kept on fasting. The devil left the pig—and then Anthony made it one more of his pets!

In many places on St. Anthony's Day, January 17, people groom their pets with bells and bows and budding flowers to honor the holy abbot. He is the patron saint of pets. Do something special for your pets this day. Give them extra attention, groom them or clean their cages or tanks.

Do all animals a favor and learn to enjoy meatless meals. Friday is the day God created humans and animals. And so we may want to take some time each Friday, like Abbot Anthony did, to thank God for creating the animals of the earth.

Memorial of St. Agnes +304,
  virgin martyr
January 21

Behold the Lamb of God

Copyright © 1991, Liturgy Training Publications, 1-800-933-1800. Written by Christine Kenny-Sheputis. Art by Suzanne Novak.

St. Agnes's Day, according to tradition, is the coldest day of the year, but cheer up! Often the "January thaw" comes during this week.

Agnes's Day falls a month after the winter solstice. This means that the daytime now is longer than it was back at Christmas. Have you noticed?

St. Agnes was a teenaged martyr. She died for her faith in Rome in the year 304, the same year that St. Lucy died. A white lamb symbolizes Agnes's purity and sacrifice. (Lambs have long been sacrificial victims.)

Agnes's lamb is a play on words: In Greek, *agnes* means pure; in Latin, *agnus* means lamb.

To remember Agnes on her day, make a white coconut pudding. Serve it with raspberry sauce as a sign of her martyrdom. You can make the pudding in the front half of a lamb-shaped pan, if you have one. Start the day before:

Mix 1¼ cups of milk, 1 cup of sugar, 1½ tablespoons of unflavored gelatin and a pinch of salt in a saucepan. Stir over medium heat to dissolve the gelatin. Chill. When slightly thickened, add 1 teaspoon of vanilla, 1⅓ cups of coconut and 2 cups of whipping cream, whipped. Fill the lamb or a ring mold and chill overnight.

To make raspberry sauce, blend 1 tablespoon of cornstarch with a 10-ounce package of thawed raspberries. Add ½ cup of currant jelly. Cook and stir until thickened and clear. Strain and cool.

Feast of the Presentation of the Lord
February 2

Candlemas is an important feast that deserves celebration at home, at school and in religious education programs, as well as in the liturgy. Perhaps that day can be something other than business as usual for all your students. Work with worship personnel to encourage students to bring their household candles to church for the blessing and procession that day.

These take-home notes would be attractive copied in Christmas colors.

Farewell to Christmas

Copyright © 1991, Liturgy Training Publications, 1-800-933-1800. Written by Christine Kenny-Sheputis. Art by Suzanne Novak.

February 2 is Candlemas, the Presentation of Jesus in the Temple. It comes 40 days after Christmas.

Today is the customary day to take down the nativity scene and to say good-bye to Christmas.

According to folklore, by February 2, even the animals begin to look forward to springtime. Wintry weather on this day is supposed to mean an early spring. And spring-like weather means winter will come back harshly. That's where the story about the groundhog comes from. If the groundhog wakes up and sees its shadow (which means the day is sunny), it goes back to sleep for 40 more days.

When Jesus was 40 days old, a man named Simeon called him "a light to the nations and the glory of Israel." So Christians celebrate Candlemas as a festival of light. In the temple, Mary and Joseph offered up two doves on this day. Today we make an offering, too. At church, there is a blessing of candles and a candlelight procession.

The blessed candles are used for ordinary times, for instance, at dinner. And they are used for special times, when anointing the sick or when communion is brought to the home.

If you bring blessed candles home from church, use them at dinner. Take one last chance to share your best memories of Christmas. With an adult's help, you can light all the other household candles from the blessed ones and enjoy the candlelight while you sing "Hark the herald angels" one last time and say good-bye to Christmas until next year.

Memorial of St. Valentine +269, martyr
February 14

On the Roman calendar, February 14 is the memorial of SS. Cyril and Methodius, brothers who were the apostles to the Slavic peoples. *Two* St. Valentine s, however, are mentioned on this day in the Roman martyrology.

Hearts and Flowers

Copyright © 1991, Liturgy Training Publications, 1-800-933-1800. Written by Christine Kenny-Sheputis. Art by Suzanne Novak.

Our St. Valentine's Day celebrations sometimes seem a far cry from honoring a priest who was martyred. And that's what St. Valentine was.

One legendary tie to St. Valentine (actually, there were *two* Valentines) is the valentine card. When one of these Valentines was in prison, he sent notes of love and encouragement to people who needed them.

Most of us know someone who needs a reminder of our love and prayers—someone who is sick, someone who once was our teacher, someone who lives alone. The pink, white and red hearts and flowers of this day will brighten anyone's winter.

If you live where there's snow on the ground, here's a fun (but messy) idea to try with an adult's help: Outside, fill a bucket or spray bottle with water. Add red food coloring. Now go "paint" the snow pink. If you're careful, you can trace a heart on a snowy lawn—just watch where you walk!

Again, with an adult's help, you can make edible valentines. Bake or buy gingerbread or sugar cookies in heart shapes. Decorate them with pink or white Cakemate icing. Squeeze hearts, ruffles, names or messages on the cooled cookies and let the icing dry. Then wrap each one in pink, white or red tissue paper and deliver them (with a note) to the lucky people.

Carnival/Shrove Tuesday/Mardi Gras

Carnival is the festive period before Lent. In some traditions, it lasts from Epiphany until Ash Wednesday. The final day of Carnival is called Shrove Tuesday (people were "shriven" or forgiven their sins on this day) and Mardi Gras (in French, literally, "Greasy Tuesday," from all the fatty foods eaten on this day).

Hand out the take-home note for Ash Wednesday during the week that Carnival and Ash Wednesday fall. Hand out the note for Carnival the week before that. Carnival colors are traditionally gold, green and purple (representing gold, frankincense and myrrh; and Easter, springtime and Lent).

Fat Tuesday

Copyright © 1991, Liturgy Training Publications, 1-800-933-1800. Written by Christine Kenny-Sheputis. Art by Suzanne Novak.

Mardi Gras *(mar-dee grah)* means "Fat Tuesday" in French. It's the day before Ash Wednesday, when Lent begins.

If we are serious about keeping Lent, the Mardi Gras party before it should be great fun. Plan all the things you will need: your favorite music, party hats and noise-makers, masks, confetti, streamers, your most favorite foods and, of course, guests.

Popular Mardi Gras foods are pancakes in Great Britain, crepes in France, stuffed grape leaves in the Middle East, sweet rice in Puerto Rico, cream rolls in Scandinavia, sausages and peppers in Italy, and doughnuts in Poland and Germany.

Pick the time and place, and invite the people. And remember—there's a point behind the party. It gets us ready to keep a good Lent. Mardi Gras is a little like emptying our drawers and closets into a pile before we straighten them out. We can wear costumes and masks to make fun of our bad habits: Draw TV screens around your eyes if you watch television too much. Draw the stopped hands of a clock on your face if you are always running late. Wear a general's medals if you are bossy.

At the end of the party, have paper and pencils ready. Write down how you want to improve during Lent. You can pass these around or talk about the help you will need to succeed. Then tear them up into tiny bits and bury them in the ground or put them in the trash. At the end, to begin Lent, join hands and say the Our Father. Then clean up in silence.

TAKE ME HOME

Ash Wednesday

Lent is the season of preparation for Easter. Through fasting, prayer and the giving of charity during the Forty Days of Lent, we prepare to renew our baptism at Easter. We prepare certain catechumens for baptism. And we lead people who have been alienated from the church back to their baptism and to unity with the church.

The word Lent means "spring." It comes from the same root as the word "lengthen," because daytime lengthens during Lent. Dark winter passes over into bright springtime.

Ash Wednesday is the first day of Lent. Holy Thursday is the final day. The first four days of Lent are a kind of "warm-up" for the season. The "Forty Days of Lent" are counted from the First Sunday of Lent (the first day) until Holy Thursday (the fortieth day).

There are handouts in this book for each week of Lent (and Eastertime, too), as well as this hand-out for the week of Ash Wednesday. Good paper colors for Lent include gray, purple, buff and brown.

Get Well Soon

On Ash Wednesday we begin Lent, a season that lasts until Easter. We wear ashes and remember how short our lives are. That may be hard to believe when you are young, but it gets easier to believe as you grow older.

The ashes help us know our place and let other people know it. We are marked with a cross—a sign of suffering and a sign of healing.

The ashes are made from the burned-up palms from last year's Palm Sunday. Outside, with an adult's help, you can burn up your old palms and then leave the ashes in a bowl in a special place during Lent. Just think—when Lent is nearly over, spring will be here and we will have fresh green palms once again!

Adults begin Lent with a fast: very skimpy meals and no food in between. It seems simple, and it is. Older children may want to join in the adult's fast. It can remind us how often we just pop things into our mouths without thinking.

We skip meat today, too, and every Friday until Easter. Long ago, it was more than meat. On every day of Lent, people did not eat meat, eggs, butter, oil or cheese. That left fish, grains, vegetables, flour and water—it was a healthier way to eat.

Nowadays, many people think that the old-fashioned lenten fast is a smart way for humans to eat. Your family can talk about ways you can keep the fast of Lent. Talk about ways to become healthier and holier by Easter.

First Sunday of Lent

Little Arms

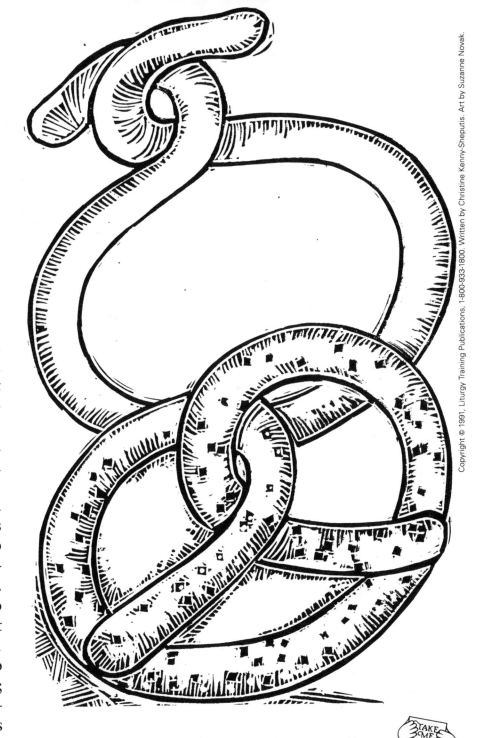

Copyright © 1991, Liturgy Training Publications, 1-800-933-1800. Written by Christine Kenny-Sheputis. Art by Suzanne Novak.

Long ago, Christians kept a strict fast all through Lent. Even their bread gave up ingredients: no eggs, butter or fat. That pretty much left yeast, flour, water and salt—simple basic bread.

Long ago, when Christians prayed, they put their right hands on their left shoulders and their left hands on their right shoulders—to form crosses. In Lent, some Christians twisted their bread into "little arms" crossed in prayer, called *"bracellae"* in Latin and "pretzels" in English. People gave pretzels to each other during Lent to remind them to stick to their fasting, prayer and alms-giving (the giving of charity) throughout the season.

Pretzels were baked on Ash Wednesday and fed believers until Easter—then disappeared again. With an adult's help, you can make lenten pretzels like this:

Grease two cookie sheets and sprinkle with salt. In a large bowl, dissolve a packet of dry yeast in 2 tablespoons of warm water. Add 1⅓ cup of warm water and ⅓ cup of brown sugar. Knead in 5 cups of flour until the mixture forms a smooth ball. Then knead 10 more minutes.

Divide the dough into 24 pieces. Roll each piece into a 14-inch strand and twist it into a pretzel shape. Heat the oven to 475˚. Fill a large skillet with water, adding 1 tablespoon of baking soda for each cup of water. Bring to a simmer. With a spatula, lower a pretzel into the water; cook 30 seconds. Transfer to a cookie sheet and sprinkle with salt. Repeat with each pretzel. Bake 8 minutes until golden.

Second Sunday of Lent

A Place for Prayer

Copyright © 1991, Liturgy Training Publications. 1-800-933-1800. Written by Christine Kenny-Sheputis. Art by Suzanne Novak.

Y ou can pray anywhere. You can pray while washing your face, while riding a bus, while sitting in the library. Every place is a holy place.

But sometimes it is good to prepare a special place for prayer. There you can put reminders that, as a Christian, you never pray alone. You pray through Christ, with Christ, in Christ—in the company of all the angels and saints.

If you do not already have a prayer corner at home, give it some thought. It doesn't need to be big. Part of a desk, a shelf, a small table or the top of a bedroom dresser is fine. There should be space for a picture or a cross or a statue.

You may want to add a bowl of water to sign yourself each morning to remember your baptism. Keep a prayer book and the Bible nearby. As the seasons change and special days come, you can put your Advent calendar there, your nativity scene, blessed palms and pussy willows, Easter eggs, a Pentecost dove and other reminders of your faith.

This will be a place to pray—to talk to God, to Mary and to the saints. It will be your own or your family's place to give praise and thanksgiving, to ask for forgiveness and to ask for help. Use it at ordinary times, special times, private times. And use it regularly. Prayer is a habit, a good habit to get into this Lent that can last a lifetime.

TAKE ME HOME

Third Sunday of Lent

A Holy Diet

Copyright © 1991, Liturgy Training Publications, 1-800-933-1800. Written by Christine Kenny-Sheputis. Art by Suzanne Novak.

During Lent, we take a long, hard look at a few ordinary activities: choosing, cooking and eating food. This is the season when many farm animals give birth to their babies. Then they nurse their young on milk. It's a time of year when birds lay eggs and wait for the eggs to hatch. By eating less meat or eggs or milk for a few weeks—which is an old tradition during Lent—we can help a new generation of animals get off to a healthy springtime start.

In many places in the world today, late winter and early spring is a time when the foods that people stored during the past fall begin to run out. So everyone fasts together. That helps the food last longer. It can help all the people to survive.

Even if we can buy food any time from a supermarket, fasting together during Lent can remind us that we must care for each other. We need to keep all hungry people in mind. We are all living on this planet together. What one person does eventually affects everybody. The earth is like Noah's ark.

So every Lent, for 40 days we are very careful to watch what we eat. We streamline our eating to give more time to prayer and charity. The good of our fellow humans, the good of our souls and the good of our planet make strong motives.

Memorial of St. Patrick +c461, bishop
March 17

Solemnity of St. Joseph +1st century,
husband of Mary
March 19

Add this take-home note for SS. Patrick and Joseph to the lenten weekly note. The obvious color for the paper is a springtime green, good for both saints.

Lenten Saints

Copyright © 1991, Liturgy Training Publications, 1-800-933-1800. Written by Christine Kenny-Sheputis. Art by Suzanne Novak.

Two saints' days interrupt our lenten fasting with festivity—St. Patrick on March 17 and St. Joseph on March 19. It is customary to eat fish on both days, maybe to remind us that it is still Lent and maybe as a symbol for Christ. The first letters of the Greek words for "Jesus Christ, the Son of God, the Savior" spell the Greek word for fish, *ichthus*.

St. Patrick's true fans start his day with Mass—then fill it with bagpipes and dancing, parades and wearing the shamrocks he used when he talked about the Holy Trinity to the people who were preparing for baptism at Easter.

Green is worn this day to welcome springtime. Long ago, people wore green on Holy Thursday for the same reason. That was the day that people who were separated from the church because of their sins were united once again in time for Easter.

St. Joseph, Jesus' foster father, is the patron of foster families. A special custom on his solemnity is a "St. Joseph's Table." A large table is set beautifully with linens and dishes. A picture or statue of Joseph is placed at the head of the table with its own place setting. The family or community of neighbors prepares and serves the best lenten meatless foods to poor, lonely and hungry people in honor of St. Joseph.

On a smaller scale, families can prepare a special meal and invite just one or two people who need the food, the welcome and the companionship.

TAKE ME HOME

Solemnity of the Annunciation of the Lord
March 25

The Annunciation is a great solemnity that deserves celebration at home and in the classroom. Both St. Joseph's Day and this day may at first seem more in keeping with Advent than with Lent. It might seem odd to our way of thinking, but in the earliest centuries of the church, Easter also was a celebration of the conception of Christ. Surely, the springtime brings to mind all types of births and beginnings. Particularly in Lent, we fix our attention on the people in the parish who are soon to be born anew at Easter in the "womb" of baptism.

Add this take-home note for Annunciation Day to the appropriate lenten weekly note. Springtime green is a good color for this note.

Hail Mary, Full of Grace!

March 25, Annunciation Day, is nine months *until* Christmas. And it is three months *since* Christmas. For the past three months, the nights have grown shorter and the days have grown longer. The word "Lent" comes from the word "lengthen," because days keep growing longer during Lent.

On March 20 or 21, day and night are equal in length, but by March 25, the day is longer than the night. Light conquers the darkness. And we welcome the day that the archangel Gabriel appears to Mary to announce that she will become the Mother of God.

Air and wind are symbols of the Holy Spirit. On Annunciation Day, it is traditional to eat foods that have been whipped and fluffed up with air. Mashed potatoes may be nice on this day. A lemon meringue pie may be even nicer. We celebrate the Spirit who filled Mary with God's life-giving breath.

Swedish custom calls for waffles and whipped cream today. To keep the full custom, collect leftover waffle crumbs and bury them in the garden or in a flowerpot— or scatter them outside for the newly returned robins. We do this in the hope that the same inspiring grace that made Mary fruitful will bring gardens to blossoming life.

People in the Philippines and in Greece go kite flying today. Folks in Jamaica hop on their sailboats. What other ways can you use the March wind to be inspired with the Holy Spirit on Annunciation Day?

Fourth Sunday of Lent

The middle of Lent is Laetare (Rejoice) Sunday. The rose color traditionally associated with this day is a softening of Lent's violet. The rose color calls to mind springtime flowers (this Sunday often falls near the vernal equinox). After this Sunday, Lent deepens. All eyes turn to Easter.

Alms for the Poor

Copyright © 1991, Liturgy Training Publications, 1-800-933-1800. Written by Christine Kenny-Sheputis. Art by Suzanne Novak.

We are halfway through Lent, in the middle of our journey to Easter. One key part of Lent is almsgiving—which means giving money or necessities to people who need them.

The word "alms" comes from the Greek word for "compassion." The word compassion means "to try to feel what someone else is feeling." Showing compassion for people takes a lot of practice. That is why almsgiving is best done daily. It also is best done in secret. And it is going to cost you something: a soft drink, a snack, a movie, a game, your time, your patience, your planning.

Choose something important to you. Then, in an envelope, a box or a bank, set aside the money it would have cost. The place where you put your money is called an alms box.

A piggy bank is a traditional alms box for Lent. You add money to it every day during the season. The piggy reminds people that ham and sausages come on Easter Sunday. On Holy Thursday—which is the day Lent ends—the bank is cracked open and the money brought to church for the special collection for the poor.

No matter what you use as an alms box for Lent, collect alms as often as you can until Holy Thursday. Then take it all where it can do some good: perhaps your parish poor box, Catholic Charities or the St. Vincent de Paul Society. To help people in other countries, perhaps your family can get a money order and send it to: Catholic Relief Services, 209 West Fayette Street, Baltimore, Maryland 21201.

TAKE ME HOME

A Tree of Life

Prepare an Easter tree to grace your home with new life from "dead" wood. Get a friend or a brother or sister to help. Find some bare branches or an unwanted sapling in your yard. (Be sure to get permission before cutting down any plant.)

Cut branches from the tree or bush, take them inside and put them in water. Add a couple of *drops* of bleach to the water to keep it pure. A tree stand or a big leakproof pot can help hold the branches upright. Small pebbles added to the pot also can help.

Between now and Easter, prepare bows, make yarn chicks and bunnies, cut out paper eggs, find a string of holiday lights and any other signs of new life and resurrection that you can think of.

Using construction paper, some people make figures of the famous people in the Bible whose stories we tell at Easter: Adam and Eve, Noah (and all the animals aboard the ark—and the rainbow, too), Abraham and Sarah, Isaac and Rebekah, Miriam and Moses, Esther, Judith, Jonah, Jeremiah, Daniel (and the lions, too), and the three children in the fiery furnace (the story is found in the Book of Daniel). Be sure to include the people we hear about when we tell the story of the death, burial and resurrection of Jesus.

The cross of Jesus is a tree of life. The life of the world hangs on its dead wood. On Good Friday you can put the cross in the center of your bare Easter tree. On Holy Saturday, decorate your tree carefully. Leave it up for 50 days until Pentecost.

Copyright © 1991, Liturgy Training Publications, 1-800-933-1800. Written by Christine Kenny-Sheputis. Art by Suzanne Novak.

TAKE ME HOME

Palm Sunday of the Passion of the Lord

Because this take-home note deals with preparing for Palm Sunday, it might be best to hand it out at least a week earlier. The red of the vestments and the green of the branches are colors associated with this day.

All types of branches in addition to palms may be blessed at the Palm Sunday liturgy. Work with parish worship personnel so that people will be made welcome to carry backyard branches from home to the church.

Welcome the Passover!

In desert countries such as Egypt, Lebanon and Israel, date palms are important trees. They thrive on intense heat. For dates to ripen, they need several months with temperatures over 100. It's no wonder that palm trees are symbols of eternal life!

Over the centuries, Jews, Christians and Muslims have placed palm branches on graves as promises of resurrection. John's gospel tells us that the people carried palms to welcome Jesus into Jerusalem. Jesus is like a palm tree. Jesus gives us the promise of eternal life.

In northern Europe, pussy willows are symbols of life. They are some of the first plants to spring into bloom after the long winter. Some people call willows "palms," and they bring willows to church on Palm Sunday. In every country, to welcome Jesus into Jerusalem, people bring to church whatever happens to be springing to life in their own backyards.

You can help welcome Jesus. What plants are coming to life in your neighborhood? With permission, maybe you can cut a few springtime branches from a yard or field to bring to church for the blessing. A bundle of branches can be gathered at the bottom like a tall bouquet, as people do in Guatemala. Decorate your home grown "palm tree" with ribbons and flowers, as people do in Germany.

On Palm Sunday afternoon, your fancy "palm tree" can be hung near the family cross or on the front door, or it can be carried to the cemetery to grace the graves.

TAKE ME HOME

The Paschal Triduum

The Three Days of the Death, Burial
   and Resurrection of the Lord: Holy Thursday
   evening until Easter Sunday afternoon

These three days, from Holy Thursday evening
until Easter Sunday afternoon, are the Christian
Passover. They are the most important days of the
year. They can also be the most wonderful. The
Forty Days of Lent are a preparation for these
days. The Fifty Days of Eastertime are kept in
celebration of these days.

   This take-home note can be handed out along
with the one for Palm Sunday or with the one
for Easter Sunday—given out some time before-
hand so people can use this handout to prepare
these days.

   Red, white and gold are colors associated with
the Triduum. Perhaps you can duplicate the words
of a song for people to use at home during these
holiest of holy days.

Copyright © 1991, Liturgy Training Publications, 1-800-933-1800. Written by Christine Kenny-Sheputis. Art by Suzanne Novak.

PASCHAL TRIDUUM

The Three Days of Easter

On Holy Thursday, Lent ends and the three days (the "Triduum," pronounced *trid-do-um)* of the death, rest and resurrection of the Lord begin. This is our Passover, our Easter.

From Holy Thursday evening through the Vigil of Easter, we try not to cook or work or go to school or play games or run errands. Instead, we fast, pray and keep watch. It's simple. Then the breakfast on Easter Sunday morning "breaks" our fast.

Our most powerful mysteries are celebrated during these three days. Try to be at church as much as you can— especially for the Easter Vigil, the most wonderful night of the year.

There's much that can be done at home, too:

On Holy Thursday, clean the house for Easter. Watch the sun set, then eat spring greens (like spinach) and bitter herbs (like horseradish) at dinner to welcome the Passover.

On Good Friday, fast and abstain from meat—because Adam and Eve didn't eat meat. During the Triduum we pretend we're once again in paradise. Try to keep quiet today. Set up a cross, the tree of life, in a special place. Spend time in prayer.

On Holy Saturday, continue the fast and quietness. Rest up to get ready for the holy night. Decorate your Easter tree. Color eggs. Gather flowers.

On Easter Sunday, go on an egg hunt, surprise the neighbors with treats, dress up and go visiting. Sing and thank God for creating the world, for leading slaves to freedom and for raising Jesus from the dead.

TAKE ME HOME

Easter Sunday

Easter Sunday is the third day of the Paschal Triduum. It is the solemnity of solemnities, the day of days, and it begins the Fifty Days of Easter, the happiest season of the church that lasts until Pentecost, the fiftieth day.

This handout may be sent home with the one for the Paschal Triduum and perhaps with the one for Palm Sunday, too, especially if students will not meet during the week. Schedule the distribution of these handouts so that there is time to read them and to prepare.

The handouts for Eastertime would be attractive copied on gold or pastel-colored paper.

An Eggciting Easter

Copyright © 1991, Liturgy Training Publications, 1-800-933-1800. Written by Christine Kenny-Sheputis. Art by Suzanne Novak.

Eastertime lasts for 50 days, from Easter Sunday until Pentecost. This means that we have 50 days of eggstra special celebration.

Eggs and Easter are almost inseparable. An eggshell is like Christ's tomb, harboring new life within. Play the "egg-crack game" by trying to break another person's egg with your egg—without breaking yours. Whenever you crack an Easter egg, you shout: Christ is risen!

We dye eggs every color of the rainbow to remember God's covenant with Noah and all living creatures on earth. Draw designs on eggs with wax crayons before dyeing them. The dye won't stick to the wax. With thread, tie small ferns and flowers or scraps of paper to eggs before dunking them in dye. Then remove the threads to reveal the patterns you have made.

People in Greece dye eggs red to honor Christ's blood. From the red shells emerge the white and gold of resurrection. You can dye eggs a deep, bloody red using brown onion skins. With an adult's help, hard-boil eggs for 30 minutes or longer in a pot of water stuffed with as many onion skins as you can fit in. The longer they boil, the deeper the color gets.

Early in the morning, women went to the garden where Jesus was buried to embalm his dead body. But an angel appeared and asked the women, "Why do you seek the living among the dead?" An Easter egg hunt in a garden can be like the women's search for Jesus. Instead of death, we find life.

TAKE ME HOME

Second Sunday of Easter

Eastertime is a 50-day-long season from Easter Sunday until Pentecost. This time is the longest church season and the most ancient, too. In addition to the wonderful signs we associate with Easter, Eastertime looks like and has the feel of the many glories we associate with spring—with first communions, Mother's Day, baseball games, May crownings, picnics, kite flying, handsful of lilacs and bouquets of apple blossoms.

Eastertime is a "week of weeks" plus a day— seven times seven plus one. The span of 50 days is a symbol of eternity. During Eastertime, we "play heaven," living as if God's reign is fully here, as if the world was at peace and all people enjoyed lives of justice, goodwill and abundance. Eastertime is a rehearsal for eternity.

Unless a Grain of Wheat Is Buried . . .

Grains—wheat, rice, barley, oats, corn—are powerful symbols of life, death and resurrection. During the Three Days of Easter, Good Friday to Easter Sunday, we followed the death, burial and resurrection of Jesus. Jesus was like a grain of wheat that was buried in the earth. Jesus rose to new life. In all of us who are baptized, one grain becomes a hundred grains.

On the second Monday of Eastertime, Greek farming families celebrate *colyva*. This also is celebrated 40 days after a funeral. To greet the resurrection, Greeks boil wheat until it is tender and plump, then they mix in raisins, almonds and sesame seeds. This mixture is called a pilaf. It is heaped on a platter, decorated with candied fruit and flowers, and circled with fragrant, fresh herbs.

Make your own *colyva* with a package of wheat or rice pilaf from the grocery. Follow box directions and add ½ cup of raisins, ½ cup of slivered almonds and ½ cup of sesame seeds. Mound on a platter and decorate with dried apricots, apples, dates, candied cherries or pineapple. To finish, circle the platter with fresh mint from the garden or basil and rosemary from the supermarket.

Some people use silver cake decorations, called "dragees," to form a cross on the *colyva*. Many Greek families bring *colyva* and Easter eggs to the cemetery, where they have a picnic to bring the good news of Easter to all who sleep there like planted grain, and who are waiting for the resurrection.

Copyright © 1991, Liturgy Training Publications, 1-800-933-1800. Written by Christine Kenny-Sheputis. Art by Suzanne Novak.

Easter Mischief

Easter Sunday kicked off 50 days of feasting and celebration until Pentecost.

Try an old custom. Get some water blessed during the Easter Vigil from your church. There usually is a fountain or small tank with a spout somewhere in the church. If you cannot find this Easter water, any fresh water will do just fine.

Add a drop or two of fragrant oil (from a health food store) or add an extract (vanilla, lemon, almond or orange) to the water, and sprinkle or spray it on friends and family when it is least expected. Remember to say, like the Hungarians do, "May you never wither!"

It is part mischief and part blessing, and a tame version of the dousings with whole buckets of water that are popular in eastern Europe. At Easter, a whole town can get wet. This custom dates back a thousand years to the time when the people first accepted the Christian faith. Just about everyone was baptized at Easter in ponds and rivers.

Maybe that is why water pistols appear in the stores at Eastertime: Ever since the Hebrew slaves marched through the Red Sea to freedom, there is something deep down inside of us that wants to celebrate water in the springtime. Water cleans. Water drowns. Water refreshes. Water quenches thirst. In spring, water can come in gentle showers and in terrible floods.

During Eastertime, keep a small bowl of Easter water in your prayer space, and sign yourself with the cross each day to remember and to rejoice in your baptism.

May Shrines

Copyright © 1991, Liturgy Training Publications, 1-800-933-1800. Written by Christine Kenny-Sheputis. Art by Suzanne Novak.

Eastertime always includes May, Mary's month. And that means Eastertime always includes an encounter with Mary, the Mother of God.

Mary stood by the cross when her son Jesus died. She was the first of the faithful disciples. She was a witness. And now, with the coming of Easter, she is *regina caeli (ray-gee-na chay-lee),* the queen of heaven.

All year long, the prayer corner in your home can be a candle and water bowl on a shelf, dresser or table, perhaps with a cross and even a bowl of sand for burning charcoal and incense.

For Eastertime, you can cover this place with any springtime-colored cloth, add a small pitcher or vase to hold flowers or greens, add the household's Easter candle (although the candle might be left on the dining table) and also keep nearby a book of prayers to explore a few minutes each day.

As springtime moves along during Eastertime, search for flowers to grace your prayer corner. Pay close attention to what blooms in your neighborhood. Maybe you can plant flowers, too.

In May, at the center of your prayer corner, set an image of Our Lady. If not a statue, then set a framed print, a holy card or a reproduction of her image from an art book. If you are artistic, create another image. Maybe you want to make a new image of Our Lady each year to add to a collection.

Any way you do it, make a place, and Mary's presence will fill it day by day as you offer your praise and prayers and devotion.

Fifth Sunday of Easter

Our Easter Zoo

Copyright © 1991, Liturgy Training Publications, 1-800-933-1800. Written by Christine Kenny-Sheputis. Art by Suzanne Novak.

The church's seasons are surrounded by legends. These are gifts of imagination to our Christian faith. The most imaginative Eastertime legends are about mythological animals that are symbols of our risen Lord.

There is the *unicorn,* the one-horned animal that laid down its life for the innocent. There is the *hydra,* the many-headed serpent that was swallowed whole by the jaws of a giant crocodile. But then, to free itself, the hydra munched away at the crocodile from inside!

There is the *pelican,* the seabird that feeds its babies from its own blood. There is the *phoenix,* the splendid bird of paradise that burned up in the fronds of a palm tree. But the next morning, the phoenix rose from its ashes back to life, more beautiful than it was before.

Sin and death often are imagined as great scaly dragons, named *Leviathan* or *Basilisk* or *Behemoth.* Lord Jesus slays death's dragon and turns it into the first course of the heavenly banquet. Imagine that! Heaven might be like a fish fry.

Is it any wonder that St. George, whose feast day is April 23, is the patron saint of Eastertime? According to legend, George battled with a dragon and won the victory. His name means "farmer." Our Easter barnyard has more to offer than chickens, rabbits and ducks!

TAKE ME HOME

Sixth Sunday of Easter

Solemnity of the Ascension of the Lord

Firstfruits of Easter

Copyright © 1991, Liturgy Training Publications, 1-800-933-1800. Written by Christine Kenny-Sheputis. Art by Suzanne Novak.

On the fortieth day of Eastertime, always a Thursday, we celebrate the solemnity of the Ascension, when Christ returns to his Father and passes his work on to the apostles. The church continues the celebration during the following weekend.

An old custom is to bless the firstfruits of the spring season on Ascension Day—as Jesus blessed the apostles, the firstfruits of his labor.

If you have a garden, and things are growing, harvest a few of the "firstfruits" of springtime—vegetables, herbs or flowers. This time of year it is not unusual for parsley to be coming up, and rhubarb, and maybe even the first peas and strawberries. If you do not have a garden, choose something from the produce department that you haven't eaten yet this spring.

Before dinner, gather everyone for the blessing:

> Bless, O Lord, these new fruits that you have brought to maturity by the dew of heaven, by plentiful rains and by tranquil and favorable weather. You have given us this food for our use that we may receive it with thanks in the name of Jesus Christ, who is Lord for ever and ever. Amen.

Picnics are customary for Ascension Day and throughout Eastertime, when we may want to wander outdoors and do some cloud gazing. So plan to enjoy dinner outdoors if you can or have a meal picnic-style on the living room floor if you can't get out.

TAKE ME HOME

Seventh Sunday of Easter

Unbabbling Babel

Copyright © 1991, Liturgy Training Publications, 1-800-933-1800. Written by Christine Kenny-Sheputis. Art by Suzanne Novak.

The proud people of the city of Babel decided to build an enormous tower, one so big that it would go straight up to heaven. God saw them building this tower and decided to put a stop to it. Suddenly, everyone who was working on the tower spoke a different language. (Imagine how confusing it was!) And the tower of Babel never was completed.

On Pentecost, what happened at Babel is reversed. The Holy Spirit comes down and teaches everyone one language—the good news! God's Holy Spirit is like a tower to help us walk into heaven.

On Pentecost, we celebrate the "seven gifts" of the Holy Spirit: wisdom, understanding, counsel, strength, knowledge, piety and respect. And we celebrate the "twelve fruits" of those gifts: charity, joy, peace, patience, benignity, goodness, endurance, mildness, faith, modesty, continence and chastity. Look up these words in the dictionary. They are all old-fashioned virtues. And old-fashioned virtues are powerful and rare in today's world.

Make a mobile to hang in the dining room. The mobile can have seven paper doves on which are written the seven gifts, and it can have twelve paper flames on which are written the twelve fruits of the Spirit.

New fruits coming into season are perfectly timed for a "twelve-fruit salad." Choose your twelve favorites to serve drizzled with a dressing of honey, fresh lime juice and a pinch of ginger mixed to taste.

TAKE ME HOME

Solemnity of Pentecost

Pentecost is the grand finale of Eastertime; it is the fiftieth and final day of the season. Pentecost is one of the greatest days on the church's calendar. Educators have a responsibility to foster enthusiasm for a truly popular celebration of this splendid day.

The days between Ascension and Pentecost are the original "novena," a Latin word meaning "nine days." These days are devoted to prayer and preparation for Pentecost. The take-home notes for the Seventh Week of Easter and for Pentecost both focus on preparations for this great day.

"Hot" colors are associated with Pentecost— bright pinks, reds and oranges. Perhaps the take-home note for this day can be joined to a copy of the words of a Pentecost song to sing at home.

PENTECOST

A Fiery Finale

On Pentecost, we celebrate the coming of the Holy Spirit. Eastertime ends with the sound of wind, tongues of fire, instant understanding and enough Spirit to launch a church.

Celebrate the fire of the Spirit. Wear fire colors on Pentecost: oranges, reds, hot pinks. Pass around sparklers. Invite the neighbors to a barbecue. Celebrate the wind of the Spirit: Hang wind chimes, wind socks, flags and mobiles, or go fly a kite!

At Christmas, many people decorate their homes with evergreens; at Easter, people use flowers. At Pentecost, it's the custom to decorate the house with fresh, green branches, grasses and reeds to welcome the summer. Pentecost flowers are fragrant roses, irises, poppies and peonies—or any flower with a delicious aroma.

On Saturday, Pentecost Eve, get together ingredients for Sunday's dessert: 30 large strawberries, washed and dried, 1 regular box of instant vanilla pudding, 1 cup of milk, ½ of a pint of whipping cream and 1 orange.

On Sunday, before dinner, combine the pudding mix and the 1 cup of milk, and blend. Whip the cream and fold into the pudding. Grate the orange peel onto a sheet of waxed paper.

Line up the strawberries, point up, and cut an X halfway down. With a spoon, fill the Xs with pudding, mounding it over the top. Sprinkle each with the grated peel, and refrigerate until serving.

Copyright © 1991, Liturgy Training Publications, 1-800-933-1800. Written by Christine Kenny-Sheputis. Art by Suzanne Novak.

Keeping Holy the Lord's Day

Every Sunday can be a day of renewal and reunion: with our God, with our church, with our families, with ourselves.

On weekdays, there is usually some role required of us: to be a student, an athlete, a club member. But on Sundays, we put aside our roles for a day. We have permission—even a command—to celebrate the most important things we believe: eternal life and the triumph of love.

Some people make a special effort on Sundays *to avoid* doing certain things. This is a rehearsal for the rest of the week. We can avoid squabbling, overeating or trying to do too much.

Many people try to avoid shopping on Sundays. It is good to keep at least one day of the week free from spending money. Money is important. But money gets to be too important sometimes. Sunday can be the day that we remind ourselves that many other things are far more important than money. What are they?

Some people make a special effort on Sundays *to do* certain things. They go to worship together. They eat a big breakfast. They promise their families that they will all enjoy supper together. They spend Sunday afternoons doing something that refreshes the brain as well as the body—such as taking a trip to a zoo, playing musical instruments together or going to a garden to learn the names of different trees.

How will you keep the Lord's Day? Every week, we have a fresh chance to rejoice in "the day that the Lord has made."

Copyright © 1991, Liturgy Training Publications, 1-800-933-1800. Written by Christine Kenny-Sheputis. Art by Suzanne Novak.

TAKE ME HOME

**Solemnity of the Body and Blood
of Christ**

Planting Paradise

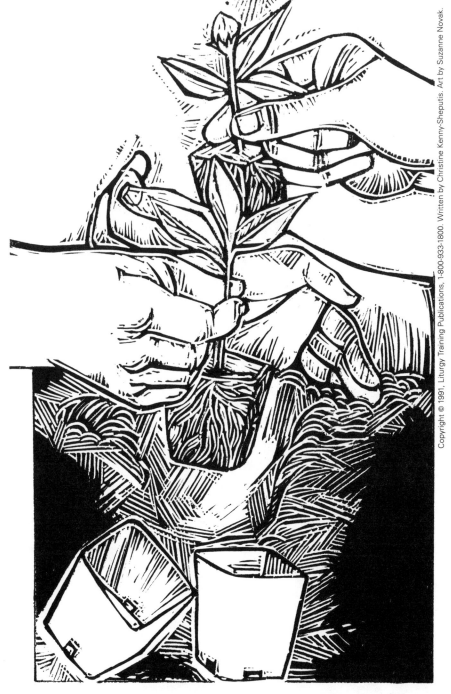

Copyright © 1991, Liturgy Training Publications, 1-800-933-1800. Written by Christine Kenny-Sheputis. Art by Suzanne Novak.

Before we can grow grain to make bread, or grapes to make wine, or any fruit or vegetable or flower, we must plant them and keep them tended throughout the summer.

Do you have a garden? It can be simple, such as a flowerpot. Or it can be as big as paradise—God's garden. Flowers that are easy to grow from seeds planted now in a sunny spot are nasturtium *(nas-tur-shum),* cleome *(clee-oh-me)* and cosmos. Nasturtium seeds are big, like peas. Cleome seeds are tiny, like black pepper. Cosmos seeds are in between.

After you plant the seeds (follow the directions on the packages), keep them watered every day until they come up. Weeds will come up, too. Get rid of the weeds. Thin the flower seedlings by pulling out extras, so the ones remaining are at least five inches apart. This feels wasteful, but flowers will not grow well if they are crowded.

Or get some gladiolus bulbs at a garden shop. For each bulb, dig a hole six inches deep. Place the bulbs pointy-side up, cover completely with dirt and pat firm. As long as you will be on your knees, whisper a brief blessing or prayer over them.

Then wait patiently. In a few weeks, the shoots will emerge. By August, maybe by Assumption Day, when we celebrate Mary's welcome into heaven, a little bit of God's kingdom will bloom in glorious colors. If this is what happens to brown little bulbs, imagine what's waiting for us on the day of resurrection!

Mother's Day
Second Sunday in May

Mother's Day always falls during Eastertime. Hand out this take-home note along with the appropriate note for the week in Eastertime.

Copyright © 1991, Liturgy Training Publications, 1-800-933-1800. Written by Christine Kenny-Sheputis. Art by Suzanne Novak.

Honor Your Many Mothers

While we are celebrating Eastertime, it is a very good season to celebrate our mothers, who have brought us into life and who can teach us to begin living eternal life.

There as so many mothers to honor—grandmothers, godmothers, adoptive mothers, stepmothers, foster mothers, den mothers and friends' mothers. There's Mary, the Mother of God. We honor Mary throughout Eastertime because, according to John's gospel, Jesus made Mary the mother of all baptized people. And, of course, there's Mother Earth. This title for our planet is one way of saying that God has made the Earth a holy home for all living things. In different ways, any one or more of these mothers has earned our love.

Write (or tape record) a very special story or letter to your mother. Think of the nicest things she has done for you—holding you when you cried at night, making pancakes with faces, bringing you hot chocolate when you didn't even ask, or taking you someplace special.

Be sure to write or record those things with all the details that you can remember. Don't forget to say how it felt when she did them and how you still feel about them now. Maybe you can add your own drawings and think up other ways to decorate your letter or recording.

Wrap the letter or recording and tie it with a ribbon. With a handful of dandelions or violets or maybe even a few lilacs, give it to her on Mother's Day.

TAKE ME HOME

Father's Day
Third Sunday in June

June 24, the Solemnity of the Birth of John the Baptist, falls during the week after Father's Day; in this book, there is a take-home note for this important solemnity. Perhaps the two take-home notes can be given out at the same time.

Tell Me a Story

Copyright © 1991, Liturgy Training Publications, 1-800-933-1800. Written by Christine Kenny-Sheputis. Art by Suzanne Novak.

The National Conference of Catholic Bishops put together a wonderful book that belongs in every Catholic home: *Catholic Household Blessings and Prayers.* Among its many treasures, this book has a special blessing for fathers that can be used at dinner on Father's Day.

In the gospels, we read how Jesus used parables to teach the people. Parables are stories that seem simple at first. But the more you think about them, the more you can learn.

Our own fathers and all those who "father" us have parables to share. It is up to the Spirit working in us to help us understand that these stories are parables. They are lessons on the ways of heaven.

When you celebrate Father's Day this year, ask your father or anyone who has been a father to you to share some special stories—especially about times when he really felt like a father. Then tell your father a story about the good things that he has done and how he has affected your life.

Take time to write down some of these stories. Be sure you do this in a notebook or diary or in something that is more sturdy than loose papers are. You can give your father these stories on the next Father's Day, or on his birthday, or whenever you have them finished.

These "parables" can be a gift to your father that no necktie can rival.

Solemnity of the Birth of St. John the Baptist
June 24

The Birth of John the Baptist (Midsummer Day) is a great festival of the church, one that deserves full celebration at home and in the parish. Religious educators can use this day, which falls after the close of the school year, as a "grand finale" to their work and as a kick-off to summer vacation.

This is a well-timed day to hold a celebration that brings together the students who participated in the religious education program and their families, the parochial school children and any other participants in parish religious education.

The Midsummer Nativity

Copyright © 1991, Liturgy Training Publications, 1-800-933-1800. Written by Christine Kenny-Sheputis. Art by Suzanne Novak.

June 24 is the birth of St. John the Baptist. This day is called Midsummer Day because we are halfway between the beginning of spring and the beginning of autumn.

Six months ago we celebrated the birth of Christ. A half year has gone by. Now we celebrate another birth. St. John's Day sometimes is called "Summer Christmas."

John the Baptist said, "Christ must increase, but I must decrease." What do you think John meant? Ever since Christmas, daytime has been growing longer and nighttime shorter. But now that summer is here, daytime begins to grow shorter and nighttime longer. Like John the Baptist, daytime is decreasing, too.

Jesus is called the light and John is called the lamp that holds the light. At baptism, we received the light of Jesus. We became lamps! Long ago, nighttime bonfires in honor of St. John were set blazing. Maybe that is why fireworks are so popular this time of year. Even fireflies seem to be celebrating with their own little lamps. Some people set out *luminarias* (paper bags with sand in the bottom and a lit candle inside) to light a path to their front door to "prepare the way of the Lord."

Even if your "bonfire" is in a barbecue grill, bless it on St. John's Day with these words:

> O God almighty, unfailing ray and source of all light, sanctify this fire that we have kindled in joy at the birth of John, the herald of your Son, and grant that, after the darkness of this life, we may come to you, who are light eternal. Amen.

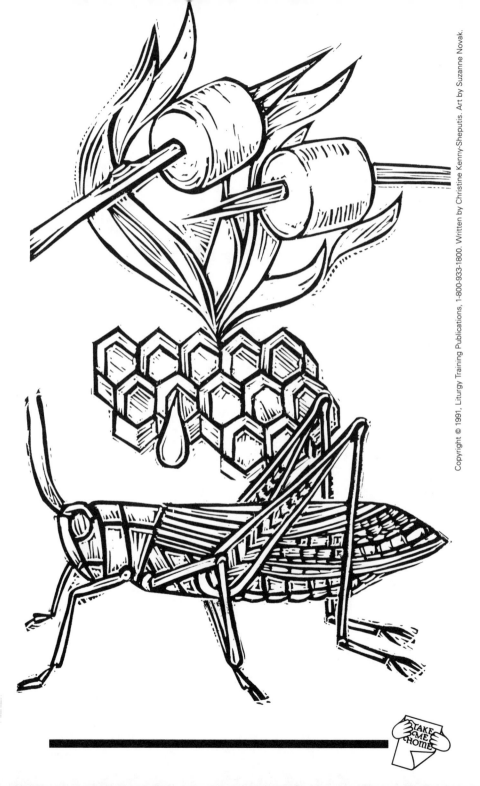

Solemnity of SS. Peter and Paul
    +1st century, apostles
June 29

Give Us This Day Our Daily Bread

Most people think about the harvest in autumn, especially around Thanksgiving. But the harvest begins now, in June. This is the time of year that the "amber waves of grain"—barley, wheat and oats—begin to ripen on the plains of North America and in the plains of Russia and the Ukraine, too.

The church celebrates the beginning of the harvest with the Solemnity of SS. Peter and Paul—apostles, missionaries and martyrs. These two saints are remembered together for beginning the "harvest of the church." We all are part of that harvest. We are God's grain.

St. Peter enjoys many popular customs, especially in fishing communities. (Peter was a fisherman.) In many countries, there is a waterfront parade of newly painted and ribbon-bedecked boats. Of course, a lunch of seafood follows.

St. Paul might well be toasted with a glass of grape juice. He recommended it to Timothy in his epistle: "Take a little for your stomach's sake."

One way to remember both apostles on this day is to share a really special loaf of bread. Surprise someone with fresh bread today. Plan a family trip to watch those "amber waves of grain."

When grain is ready to harvest, rain or wind or hail can easily ruin it. Say a prayer for all who help in "bringing in the sheaves."

Copyright © 1991, Liturgy Training Publications, 1-800-933-1800. Written by Christine Kenny-Sheputis. Art by Suzanne Novak.

TAKE ME HOME

Independence Day
July 4

Independence Day in America is not a religious observance, and it should not be made one. It is, however, a beloved national holiday and a fitting occasion for prayer, penance and thanksgiving.

The summertime take-home notes in this book may be handed out in a batch at the end of the school year, or they may be useful to vacation Bible schools or other religious education that continues during summer vacation. Educators may consider mailing these notes along with any other summertime mailings to maintain contact with students and their families.

A Day to Make Memories

Copyright © 1991, Liturgy Training Publications, 1-800-933-1800. Written by Christine Kenny-Sheputis. Art by Suzanne Novak.

How do you celebrate our national day? Do your neighbors hold a block party? Do your relatives have a picnic? Do you make homemade ice cream? How about fixing a big blueberry and strawberry shortcake as a birthday cake for our country? Or how about dressing up like one of our national heroes?

This is a great day to get to know people you don't know. You will see lots of folks if you go to a park or beach or if you go to watch fireworks. People often are in a good mood on holidays. Sometimes they are more friendly. Be more friendly yourself.

This also is a great day to create memories. You can catch up on the lives of your relatives, your friends and your family's friends. If you're going to a gathering outside, bring along something simple for everyone to have fun with, such as balsa-wood airplanes or balloons or kites and string. When this day is past, people will remember you for years to come if you are generous and unselfish and courteous.

This is a day for fireworks. Many people all over the world celebrate the summer with fireworks. It's as if we were making our own thunderstorm in the sky. One reason for fireworks is to chase away what is bad and to welcome what is good. What is bad about our country that needs chasing away? What is good that needs to be helped along? What are ways that we can make our land brighter?

**Memorial of Bl. Kateri Tekakwitha +1680,
virgin
July 14**

The Lily of the Mohawks

Copyright © 1991, Liturgy Training Publications, 1-800-933-1800. Written by Christine Kenny-Sheputis. Art by Suzanne Novak.

Kateri Tekakwitha was an American Indian. Sometimes, drawings of Kateri make her look like an Indian princess, but her real life was not so romantic.

The disease smallpox had disfigured and nearly blinded her. The word "tekakwitha" means "she who feels her way along." From Kateri's baptism at age 19 until her death at 24, her life of prayer and of caring for the sick earned her the title, "Lily of the Mohawks."

Native American Catholics from many tribes get together every August for the Tekakwitha Conference. The people talk about how they can use the riches of their Indian traditions to make them better Christians. They hold sunrise worship services and healing services, and they take part in special ceremonies to honor their ancestors.

Perhaps you have Native American ancestry. Or your ancestors might have come from some place other than North America. How can you learn more about your ancestors? What special things did your ancestors do that you also can do? Can any of these traditions make you a better Christian?

One custom of the American Indians is to burn cedar boughs as a kind of incense. You can do this, too. Outside, after a barbecue with your family, when the fire is dying down, put a few fronds of juniper or cedar on the coals. The fragrant smoke is like a prayer rising up to heaven.

TAKE ME HOME

Memorial of St. Mary Magdalene
   +1st century, apostle to the apostles
July 22

Feast of St. James +1st century, apostle
July 25

Memorial of St. Martha +1st century,
   disciple
July 29

Patrons of Summertime Hospitality

Copyright © 1991, Liturgy Training Publications, 1-800-933-1800. Written by Christine Kenny-Sheputis. Art by Suzanne Novak.

St. Mary Magdalene's Day falls on July 22. A version of her name is *Madeleine*. She is the "apostle to the apostles" because she told the other apostles that Jesus was risen from the dead.

St. James's Day is July 25. He was the first apostle to be martyred. One legend tells how his body was set adrift at sea in a boat that finally washed ashore at Compostela in Spain. Pilgrims have traveled to his shrine ever since. The pilgrims identified themselves by wearing scallop shells, and the people who saw them gave them food so they wouldn't grow hungry during their journey.

St. Martha's Day falls on July 29; she's the patron of cooks. Mary, Martha and Lazarus offered Jesus the hospitality of their home many times.

All these summer saints are patrons of hospitality—good to have in this season of vacationers. All three saints can be celebrated by baking *madeleines,* delicate shell-shaped French cakes.

Preheat the oven to 400° and butter a madeleine tin (easy to find in kitchenware shops). Melt ¾ cup of butter. Sift 1 cup plus 2 tablespoons of flour with a pinch of salt and ½ teaspoon of baking powder. Beat 3 large eggs until frothy and gradually add 1 cup of sugar. Continue beating until very thick. By hand, gently fold in the flour mixture. Stir in the melted butter, 1 teaspoon of vanilla and 1 teaspoon of freshly grated lemon rind. Fill the tins two-thirds full. Bake 10 minutes or until brown at the edges. Immediately remove from the pan and cool.

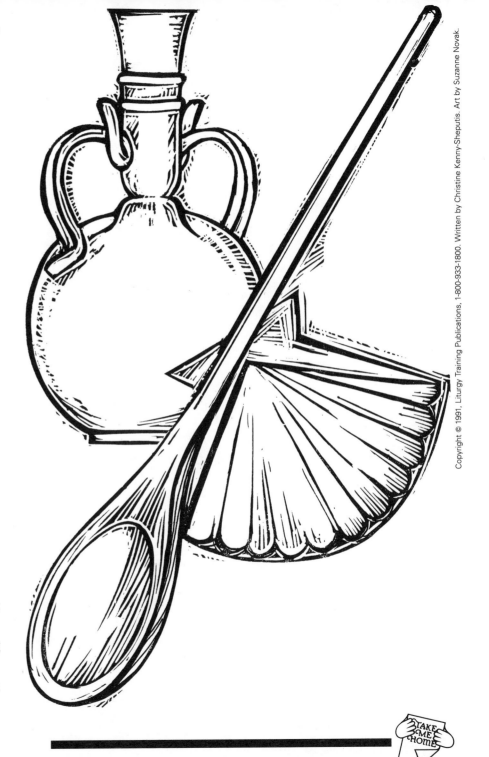

TAKE ME HOME

Feast of the Transfiguration of the Lord
August 6

This ancient feast coincides with the anniversary of the atomic bombing of Hiroshima in 1945. August 6 has become a memorial day to the first victims of nuclear war.

The people of Hiroshima use this day as a call to peace. The survivors there have become witnesses to the world of the particular horror of this kind of warfare. Perhaps they and those who died have helped the world learn ever so slowly that in this kind of warfare, all lose, all are victims.

The take-home note focuses on the church's feast. There was no room here to open up for children the memorial day of the first atomic bombing. That can be a worthy subject for discussion among children; the horror of war and the dignity of the human body are two facets of why Pope Pius XII raised the mystery of the Assumption of Mary to church dogma. Both August 6 and August 15 offer lessons on the glory of human flesh and the destiny of humankind.

Climbing
God's Holy Mountain

Copyright © 1991, Liturgy Training Publications, 1-800-933-1800. Written by Christine Kenny-Sheputis. Art by Suzanne Novak.

Our church celebrates the transfiguration of Jesus on August 6. Jesus took Peter, James and John up a mountain where he was glorified before their eyes. Moses and the prophet Elijah appeared. Then they were surrounded with a shining cloud. God's voice was heard calling Jesus "my beloved son."

Many Christians celebrate the transfiguration of Jesus by giving thanks for the bounty of the summer harvest. You might adorn your table with a gathering of August abundance from gardens and roadside stands. Leave the fruits and vegetables in place through August 15, the Assumption of Mary.

You also might end your Transfiguration Day meal with "transfigured" grain: Serve some rice pudding! Here's a recipe:

Bring 3 cups of milk and ¼ cup of converted rice to a boil. Cover and simmer slowly for 15 to 20 minutes. Remove from the heat. Preheat the oven to 350°.

Beat 4 eggs well. Add ½ cup of sugar, 1 cup of milk, 1½ teaspoons of lemon extract, 1½ teaspoons of vanilla extract and 1 tablespoon of melted butter, beating constantly.

Combine the rice and egg mixtures and pour into a buttered 8 × 8-inch pan. Sprinkle with nutmeg. Set the pan into a larger pan so the sides don't touch and add water to the larger pan. Bake about 30 minutes, then stir in ¾ cup of golden raisins. Bake 15 minutes more. Remove from the oven and cool on a rack before refrigerating.

TAKE ME HOME

Solemnity of the Assumption of Mary
August 15

This day is the most important festival of Mary. In the tradition, it was celebrated with a nightlong vigil in mourning for the death of Mary, followed by a day of celebration for her resurrection.

One title of the day is "Dormition," meaning the "Falling Asleep." The title "Assumption" is a technical term that describes Mary's being raised up into God's eternal life.

Popular celebrations of the day are titled "Our Lady of the Harvest" and "Our Lady of the Sea." All created things are blessed today in the raising of one of God's creatures into glory. The monk Thomas Merton wrote, "It is my own sister, my own flesh and blood who is assumed into heaven!"

A parish celebration is surely in order this day, complete with a blessing of garden produce. This take-home note can set the tone. Gold would be an appropriate color for the paper.

Our Lady of the Harvest

Copyright © 1991, Liturgy Training Publications, 1-800-933-1800. Written by Christine Kenny-Sheputis. Art by Suzanne Novak.

The Assumption of Mary is our church's act of faith that God has raised Mary into glory. It is a promise of eternal life made to each of us. We celebrate Mary's place as first among us to be glorified.

This feast was kept for centuries in the hearts and homes of many believers. But in 1950, Pope Pius XII claimed the feast for all Roman Catholics. It was an important way to tell the world that the human body is holy. The world needed this message after so many human bodies were destroyed in the Second World War. We are reminded by this day to treat our bodies with respect and responsibility. We have been created for glory.

Fragrant things belong to Mary—flowers and spices, potpourri and herbs. Mary's life was like a sweet smelling offering to God. On Mary's feasts, we crown her with flowers, wreathe her with roses, and festoon her shrine with herbs.

For your Assumption celebration, toast Mary with spiced herb tea. The day before, put spearmint leaves or lemon slices into ice cube trays filled with water and freeze. Boil 4 cups of water. (Children will need an adult's help.) In a teapot, put 4 chamomile tea bags; ¼ teaspoon each of orange, lemon and pineapple extracts; and a shake or two of ground cinnamon and cloves. Pour the boiling water over these ingredients. Add honey to sweeten, if you like. Cool overnight.

To serve, pour the tea over the ice cubes and toast Our Lady with a "Hail Mary."

TAKE ME HOME

**Feast of St. Bartholomew +1st century,
apostle
August 24**

St. Bart's Day

Bartholomew was one of the twelve apostles. The word "apostle" means "someone who is sent on a mission." Who sent the apostles? What was their mission?

One story says Bartholomew preached the gospel in India; another, that he went to Armenia. Can you find these countries on a globe? Almost all the stories say that Bartholomew was martyred with a scimitar—a curved sword. So he became the patron saint of anyone who works with sharp objects. These people certainly need to be extra careful in their work.

Bartholomew's late-summer feast—called "Bartlemas Day"—comes right at the time of the sheep slaughter in Europe. This day is a celebration of the "harvesting" of meat. Foot races and tests of skill are part of the fun. The feast always includes mutton roasts. (Mutton is the name of the meat from sheep.)

Have a barbecue on Bartlemas Day. Serve lamb, if you like, or another meat good for grilling. Because thanksgiving is always a big part of any harvest feast, ask each person at your feast to talk about a "harvest" that she or he is grateful for: perhaps for flowers and vegetables from the garden, a new baby in the family, a raise or promotion at work, a trip or family reunion this summer, a new friend, a successful year for the baseball team—or any blessing.

After the meal, while the barbecue coals still are hot, throw some incense over them to fill the air with the scent of celebration.

Labor Day
First Monday in September

A Labor of Love

The first Monday of September is Labor Day. And while most people think of it as the last holiday of summer, or a perfect day for a picnic, it is really much more important than that.

Labor Day is a celebration of the rights of people who work. They have a right to decent pay, to enough rest, to safe working conditions and to fair treatment. Years ago, not everyone was sure of getting these things. Even today, people struggle for their rights as workers.

This is a day to remember that people's work should dignify them, not destroy them. Over the years, many of our leaders, including the popes and bishops, have spoken out on the dignity of work and on the rights of workers.

This is a day to appreciate the work people do for you: teachers, bus drivers, coaches, farmers and cooks. The list is long. Remember your parents and other family members, too. What work do they do? And what work do you do? Today is an important day to think about the work you hope to do in years to come. You might work at many different things as the years go by.

In whatever ways you keep Labor Day, begin it in your home with this prayer from *Catholic Household Blessings and Prayers:*

God our creator, we are the work of your hands. Guide us in our work, that we may do it, not for ourselves alone, but for the common good. Make us alert to injustice, ready to stand in solidarity, that there may be dignity for all in labor and in labor's reward. Grant this through Christ our Lord. Amen.

TAKE ME HOME

Moses +12th century BCE,
**   prophet and lawgiver**
September 4

Many biblical saints have days in their honor on the Byzantine (Eastern Christian) calendar. Although these days are not found on the Roman calendar (so they are not observed in the liturgy), some biblical saints are mentioned in the Roman martyrology. For example, Adam and Eve's Day is December 24, an observance that gave rise to the custom of the Christmas "paradise tree."

Today's take-home note may be given out at the same time as the one for Labor Day. In this book, September is particularly rich with take-home notes to take advantage of the enthusiasm and energy of a new school year.

Mind Your Mannas

Copyright © 1991, Liturgy Training Publications, 1-800-933-1800. Written by Christine Kenny-Sheputis. Art by Suzanne Novak.

On the Eastern Catholic calendar, Moses the prophet is remembered on September 4.

There were so many miracles in Moses' life: He met God in the burning bush. He led the Hebrew slaves through the Red Sea to freedom. He received God's commandments on Mount Sinai.

All these wonders were dramatic—but manna was the miracle that happened every morning! Manna fed the people while they journeyed to the promised land. What was manna like? Read the Bible's description of manna in Exodus 16:31 and then try this recipe that tastes a bit like the description in the Bible. Remember: Always do your cooking or baking with an adult.

Preheat the oven to 400°. With a wooden spoon or an electric mixer, beat 1 stick of soft butter. Slowly add 1 cup of sugar, beating until it is fluffy. Add 2 eggs and beat well. Blend in 2 tablespoons of honey, ¼ teaspoon of salt and 1 teaspoon of vanilla.

In another bowl, mix 1½ teaspoons of baking powder and 2 cups of flour. Add this to the butter mixture with a wooden spoon and blend. Drop by small teaspoonfuls onto a greased cookie sheet. Place 3 coriander seeds on each (because the book of Exodus says manna tasted like coriander seeds). Bake about 8 minutes. This recipe makes 4 to 6 dozen.

Feast of the Birth of Mary
September 8

In the liturgy, three births are celebrated—Mary's, Jesus' and John the Baptist's. These are not called "birthdays" in the sense of an anniversary. These feasts are "nativities," the days of birth.

We sing at Christmas, "today is born our Savior, Christ the Lord." We sing on September 8, "let us celebrate with joyful hearts the birth of the Virgin Mary." In the liturgy, we enter into the timelessness of heaven, where the past, present and future are rolled up into one grand *now.* In mystery, the eternal enters into time, and time is swept up into eternity.

Blue, rose and gold are good paper colors for these notes.

What's in a Name?

Your "name day" is the feast day of the saint you were named for when you were baptized. When is your name day? It may take a lot of searching to find out, but it will be worth the effort.

Some families celebrate name days with as much fun as birthdays. Wake up someone on her or his name day with a big hug and kiss. Maybe you can find a book or story about the saint that the person was named after, or find a picture or statue of the saint, or draw a picture or carve a statue and make it a name-day gift.

Some people have several names. Mary, the mother of Jesus, also is called the "rose of Sharon and the lily of the valley." These names come from the Song of Songs in the Bible. September 8 is the feast of Mary's birth. Anyone named Rose or Rosa, Sharon, Lily or Lillian, Mary or any of its many variations—like Miriam, Maureen, Maria or Marirose—has a name-day celebration that day.

Make merry at the birth of Mary by placing roses by a statue or picture of her. Or have some roses for dinner! You can eat roses as long as they are free from pesticides— and free from any pests that may be along for the ride.

Freeze rosebuds into ice cubes. Decorate cream cheese sandwiches with rose petals. Float roses on gelatin. For a different drink, add a few drops of rose water to ginger ale or strawberry soda. Rose water is available in East Indian and Middle Eastern shops. You may be able to find rose-flavored ice cream in an Italian market. Or try rose-hip (berry) tea.

Feast of the Triumph of the Cross
September 14

There are 40 days between August 6 (the Transfiguration of the Lord) and the feast of the Triumph of the Cross. At one time, this was a fasting period, like Lent, to usher in a new season.

Holy Cross Day is a timely feast day to rally the parish and to begin what for many feels like a new year. The religious education program and the parochial school can get together on this.

Work with parish worship personnel to encourage everyone to bring in household crosses to bless on this day. As the take-home note explains, fragrant herbs, especially basil, are customary today. All year long, make links between home and parish.

We Should Glory in the Cross

Copyright © 1991, Liturgy Training Publications, 1-800-933-1800. Written by Christine Kenny-Sheputis. Art by Suzanne Novak.

September 14 is the feast of the Triumph of the Holy Cross. As we did a half a year ago on Good Friday, on this feast day we hold up the cross of Jesus as a sign of glory.

St. Helena lived almost 1,700 years ago (which means she lived about 300 years after Jesus). Helena was the mother of Constantine, and he was the first emperor to be baptized a Christian.

According to legend, Helena went to Jerusalem to search for the cross of Jesus. She found it on a hillside covered with basil, a green herb with a wonderful aroma. Basil is a symbol of resurrection because it sprouts in dry soil and it grows very quickly. On September 14 in the year 335, all the Christians of Jerusalem got together for the first time to honor the cross of Jesus.

Make a place for a cross in your bedroom or in your home. Use a cross from a chain or a picture or make a cross from two pieces of wood or two twigs. Or maybe you can use one of your family's crosses. You can care for it all your life and then hand it on to a young person when you grow old.

Like the Christians of Ethiopia, you might put fresh basil and other late summer herbs and wildflowers by your cross on September 14. For dessert on that day, you can bake sugar cookies cut into cross shapes, spread with chocolate frosting and perhaps decorated with silver or chocolate cake sprinkles.

TAKE ME HOME

**Feast of St. Matthew +1st century,
  apostle and evangelist**
September 21

Patron of the Unpopular

Copyright © 1991, Liturgy Training Publications, 1-800-933-1800. Written by Christine Kenny-Sheputis. Art by Suzanne Novak.

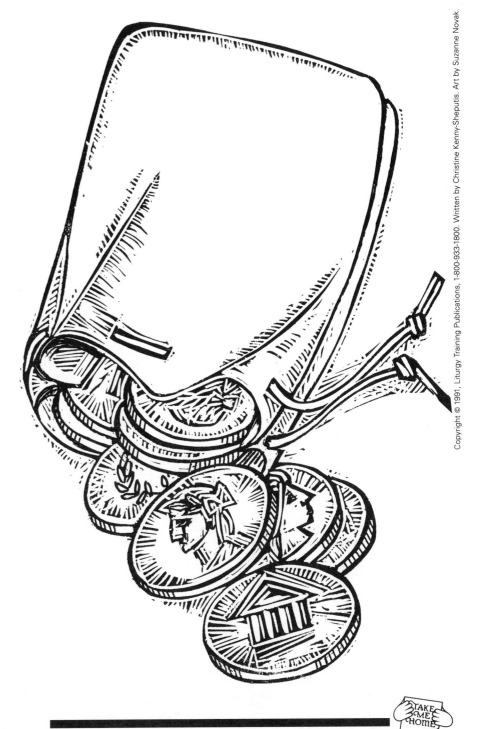

Matthew collected taxes from other people before he became an apostle. That is why Matthew is the "patron saint" of people who work with money: bankers, tax agents and financiers.

As you probably know, tax collectors sometimes aren't very popular. So Matthew is also the special patron of people who aren't well liked because of what they must do for a living.

A "patron saint" is a saint who is a good example for someone to follow. The saint can help show us how to live like a Christian in our work, in our schools and at home.

Matthew decided that money wasn't as important as what Jesus had to do. So Matthew left everything to work with Jesus. His feast day is a good time to wonder about the things and the people we think are important. What do you value most?

Sometimes our treasures multiply best when we give them away. What treasures are most worth storing away, and what treasures are worth giving away?

To remember Matthew on his day, give your family or friends chocolate coins wrapped in gold foil. Or follow an old harvest custom and use gold and silver paint or foil to decorate walnuts and almonds to share with the people who are most important to you.

TAKE ME HOME

Memorial of St. Vincent de Paul +1660, priest
September 27

Monsieur Vincent

Vincent de Paul cared for the sick. He opened schools for poor people. And he talked people who had much into helping people who had little.

Here are five good ways to connect this week with St. Vincent de Paul on his memorial day (the day the church remembers special people and events on its calendar and in the liturgy):

First, pass up something you would like to have. Vincent lived a simple life. He often gave up his own pleasures so he could afford to give to others.

Second, with a parent's help, give money or clothing or food to your parish for the poor. Many parishes support the work of the local St. Vincent de Paul Society, which does many things to help the poor.

Third, talk to your teacher about how you can invite someone from the Society to your class to talk about its work.

Fourth, check your school or public library or a video store for "Monsieur Vincent," a wonderful French movie about his life, or read about him in a book about the lives of the saints.

And fifth, remember Vincent at supper with a meal as simple as his own meals were. To a can of bean soup, add a can of water, a pinch of garlic salt, maybe a pinch of thyme and ½ teaspoonful of lemon juice. Stir and simmer. Serve with bread.

Copyright © 1991, Liturgy Training Publications, 1-800-933-1800. Written by Christine Kenny-Sheputis. Art by Suzanne Novak.

Feast of Michael, Gabriel and Raphael, archangels
September 29

Memorial of the Guardian Angels
October 2

The beginning of autumn is the time of year the church celebrates the angels in a special way. It is as if the angels are invoked to guide us through the darkness and cold of another winter.

The word angel means "messenger." It is used in the Bible for any messenger, human or divine. Christians are called to be angels of the good news. Our patrons in the proclamation of the gospel are celebrated on September 29 and October 2.

The notes for autumn in this book would look good on orange, brown, buff and gold papers.

Perhaps the words to the songs "All creatures of our God and King" and "Ye watchers and ye holy ones" (both can be sung to the same melody) can be distributed along with the take-home notes for the next few weeks. These songs seem to fit well with the autumn feasts of the church.

Michaelmas

Years ago, archangels Michael, Raphael and Gabriel were honored on separate days. Today, we celebrate them as a trio on September 29.

Most of the day's traditions center on Michael, the champion of light.

Outside some French churches, street vendors sell St. Michael's wafers. In the Hebrides Islands, St. Michael's bannocks cook on the griddles. Oatmeal pancakes have been eaten in parts of Scotland on St. Michael's Day for many centuries. Except for the fact that Scots like oatmeal, no explanation exists. In this country, some families celebrate the day with angel food cake. But the traditional food, at least in Europe, is goose. In England, onions and sage are used to stuff the bird; in Poland, sour cream and apples.

The Michaelmas goose was so deeply rooted in tradition that celebrating by roasting a goose spread to the United States in colonial times. It persists to this day in places such as eastern Pennsylvania, where, with just a nod to Michael and the angels, September 29 is observed as Good Luck Goose Day.

However simple they may seem, oatmeal pancakes, roast goose and even a slice of angel food cake can be acts of faith. They are versions of the old prayer, "St. Michael, defend us in battle!" and Jesus' own, "Deliver us from evil."

There are many, many ways to pray.

A Simple Saint

Copyright © 1991, Liturgy Training Publications, 1-800-933-1800. Written by Christine Kenny-Sheputis. Art by Suzanne Novak.

We remember St. Francis of Assisi on October 4. In his youth, Francis was rich and popular—but after a serious illness, he knew he would only be happy living the gospel in a life of simplicity, poverty and charity.

While he did much good for people, he is famous for his kindness to animals. He is also the person who created the first nativity scene, and he used living barn animals to do it.

Almost every hymnal has the song "All creatures of our God and King." Sing it today! The words are based on St. Francis's Canticle of the Sun. He called the sun, moon and stars our sisters and brothers. According to Francis, we have a very bright family. Francis called Death part of his family, too.

Who else among God's creation can you call your brother or sister? Maybe that is why we like to think of our pets as members of the family. Deep down, we are all related, from goldfish to grandparents to galaxies.

If you have pets, gather and bless them today with this prayer by Albert Schweitzer:

> O Heavenly Father, protect and bless all things that have breath. Guard them from all evil, and let them sleep in peace.

If you don't have pets (Francis didn't have pets, either), put out seeds or bread for the birds, share nuts or crackers with the squirrels or leave a little something outside for the rabbits, raccoons or opossums that travel at night.

Sukkot, the Jewish festival of harvest homes

Sukkot begins five days after Yom Kippur, the Day of Atonement, and 15 days after Rosh HaShanah, the New Year. The Jewish New Year begins at the new moon of the seventh month of the Jewish calendar. This seventh month is a holy month. Sukkot begins at the full moon in the middle of this holy month and lasts eight days. (The festival is also spelled *Sukkoth* and *Succos*.)

Perhaps the class can visit a synagogue or a Jewish center and see a "sukkah," the harvest home that is built in celebration of the festival.

Sukkot is one of the richest of Jewish festivals. Psalm 118 is the psalm of Sukkot. It is familiar from the verses, "This is the day that the Lord has made," and, "Hosannah! Blessed is the one who comes in the name of the Lord." During Sukkot, a bundle of palm, willow and myrtle branches—the *lulav*—is waved and a citron fruit—the *etrog*—is carried while the psalms are sung.

Shine on, Harvest Moon!

Copyright © 1991, Liturgy Training Publications, 1-800-933-1800. Written by Christine Kenny-Sheputis. Art by Suzanne Novak.

The full moon close to the beginning of autumn often is called the harvest moon. It seems unusually large and golden at this time of year. In the Jewish calendar, the eight-day festival of Sukkot *(soo-coat)* begins with this harvest moon. Sukkot means "harvest homes."

Long ago, when people harvested their crops, the long hours of work kept them in the fields until bedtime. Instead of going home, they put together little shacks or booths so they could sleep in the fields. They made the roofs from the crops they were harvesting. The sunlight, moonlight and starlight peeked through the spaces in the roof. Food was right at hand, and the sky was like a tent over their heads. It was like paradise.

Not many of us can sleep in a harvest home in a field, but we can bring a little of the harvest indoors to adorn our prayer corners. Collect autumn leaves of different shapes and colors, or seedpods and branches with berries. Indian corn, nuts, gourds and squashes can add color, too.

The harvest moon is also the perfect time to prepare for spring. While much of nature is shutting down and going to sleep, do something to reverse the process. Get some tulip, crocus or daffodil bulbs. Dig holes for each, about six or eight inches deep. Plant the bulbs, pointy side up, cover with earth, and water. While you're on your knees, say a prayer.

In six months, the Passover full moon will be shining in the night sky, winter will be over, and your bulbs will be in bloom.

TAKE ME HOME

Feast of St. Luke + 1st century, evangelist
October 18

Luke, the Ox

Copyright © 1991, Liturgy Training Publications, 1-800-933-1800. Written by Christine Kenny-Sheputis. Art by Suzanne Novak.

The church honors St. Luke on October 18. Luke wasn't an apostle. He was an evangelist, which means a gospel writer. He is the author of a gospel and its sequel, the Acts of the Apostles.

In this second book, Luke is called a doctor. Luke reports many stories about healing in his books. According to a legend, Luke also was an artist. Some people have said that the holy pictures in their churches were drawn by Luke. Maybe people think that Luke was an artist because his writing is colorful and includes many details.

In church symbolism, Luke is represented by an ox. This animal was used in sacrifices in the Jewish Temple. Luke's gospel begins in the Temple. Zachariah is offering a sacrifice when the angel Gabriel comes to promise him a son, John the Baptist.

Luke's feast day comes at a time of year when people prepare their meat for the winter. It is an old custom to roast an ox (or some beef) on this day to remember St. Luke. How about serving oxtail soup or some other hearty soup on this autumn day?

Of course, Luke is the patron saint of artists, writers and doctors. Spruce up your home's prayer corner with a new holy picture, maybe of your own making. Practice your reading and writing skills. Write your doctors, dentists and counselors notes of thanks for their good and important work.

TAKE ME HOME

Halloween
After sundown, October 31

Please read the suggestions for All Saints and All Souls. Halloween, All Saints and All Souls should be prepared and celebrated together.

All Hallows

Halloween is the night of October 31. The word means "Hallow's Eve." "Hallows" is another word for saints. November 1 is All Saints' Day. November 2 is All Souls' Day. Together, these days once were called "Hallowmas."

So Halloween isn't just the way we end October. It also is the way we begin November. On Halloween night—the holy eve of All Saints' Day—we begin the church's month to remember the dead.

Take time now to plan more than a costume. Start collecting pictures, letters or other reminders of relatives or friends who have died. Plan to pray for them—and with them—beginning on Halloween and then all through November. Clear a space in your bedroom or in your home to place your reminders.

If you have a small ladder or step stool, you can place a photo or letter on each step and make a "Jacob's ladder" of the people who have gone before you into heaven. Add some autumn leaves, gourds, Indian corn and other signs of the harvest. Get your family's help in doing this.

Have you ever made "grave rubbings"? Tape a large sheet of thin paper over a gravestone in a cemetery. Remove the wrapping from a crayon, then use the whole length of the crayon to rub over the paper. The carvings on the gravestone will appear on the paper. This grave rubbing makes a good memento (which means "something to remember someone by").

When you visit the cemetery, be sure to say a prayer and even sing a song to remember the people who sleep there.

TAKE ME HOME

Solemnity of All Saints
November 1

All Saints' Day is one of the premier days of the church. Halloween is not a separate celebration; rather, it is the beginning of All Saints, the holy eve of the festival. Color All Saints and All Souls with Halloween traditions and decorations.

Religious educators will want to prepare October 31 and November 1 and 2 with care. Plan activities that will bring parish children and youth together with the other generations. Work hard to see in the familiar customs of Halloween evidence of Christian faith, of hospitality and playfulness and generosity, of a healthy remembrance of the dead in anticipation of the great homecoming of heaven.

In this book, we have three take-home notes for this festival, one for Halloween, one for All Saints, one for All Souls. These three notes complement one another. They can be handed out individually week by week beginning in mid-October or they can be sent home together in late October.

Copyright © 1991, Liturgy Training Publications, 1-800-933-1800. Written by Christine Kenny-Sheputis. Art by Suzanne Novak.

When All the Saints Go Marchin' In . . .

Every good celebration needs studying and planning, and All Saints' Day, November 1, deserves lots of preparation. When you go to Mass on All Saints, remember that you are honoring the famous saints and also the quiet ones—maybe some of your own relatives.

Start by conducting some research on your patron saint. Patron saints are the success stories of our faith. They have shared our names, our hardships and our goals in this life. And many of them have left us their methods to use. You can have more than one patron. Check the library for books on the lives of the saints.

Next, do some research on family members who have died. Ask your relatives about these family members. Maybe they will let you look through photo albums. Be patient when you ask the questions—sometimes it is hard for people to talk about the dead. Maybe someone will want to talk with you a few days or even weeks after you ask a question. The conversation will be worth the wait.

Be sure to write down what people have told you. Also, keep a collection of the photos you have gathered and the items you may have collected to remember the dead. Keep these from year to year and bring them out every November. That way you, too, can share your memories with the people around you.

All Souls
November 2

All Souls is an important day for Catholics; give it full attention at home, at school, at worship and in other aspects of parish life. Coordinate efforts with other parish leaders and departments. See to it that this day is not business as usual but rather a healthy beginning to the church's November-long remembrance of the dead.

Children and the young stand to benefit from a full celebration of the church's Day of the Dead. Do not shield the young from the subject of death. If you do not present the richness of Christian attitudes, customs and practices surrounding death, the entertainment industry's attitudes and values regarding death—a favorite subject in movies and music—may predominate in the lives of students.

The take-home notes for Halloween and All Saints also are useful in celebration of All Souls.

A-Souling We Will Go!

Copyright © 1991, Liturgy Training Publications, 1-800-933-1800. Written by Christine Kenny-Sheputis. Art by Suzanne Novak.

A long history of caring unites Christians on both sides of death. An old custom for All Souls' Day, November 2, and for all of November—the month to pray for the dead—is to make "soul cakes." They are sweet, spiced dough baked in a circle. They are given away as a kind of prayer for a loved one who has died.

Doughnuts, doughnut holes or any round, sweet bun or bread can be a November soul cake. The circular shape is a symbol of heaven, where the beginnings and endings of things will run into each other.

In the old days, at this time of year, folks went from door to door promising prayers for each soul cake received. It was like the whole town was having a party. "Going a-souling" was the beginning of our North American custom of trick or treat.

To serve with soul cakes, prepare "Saints' Honey" for any souls—living or dead—who happen to drop by. Peel, core and chop a few firm, ripe pears and place them in a 2-quart pot. Add ¼ of a lemon, sliced thin, 1¼ cups of sugar, ½ teaspoon of ginger, a pinch of nutmeg and ½ cup of water. Boil 12 to 15 minutes until the mixture looks like jam. Pour into a jar.

Before bed, leave doughnuts and some apple cider out on a napkin to refresh some soul in transit during November's long nights. On Halloween, All Saints and All Souls, try this old custom with your family or friends. And don't forget to pray the prayers your soul cakes represent.

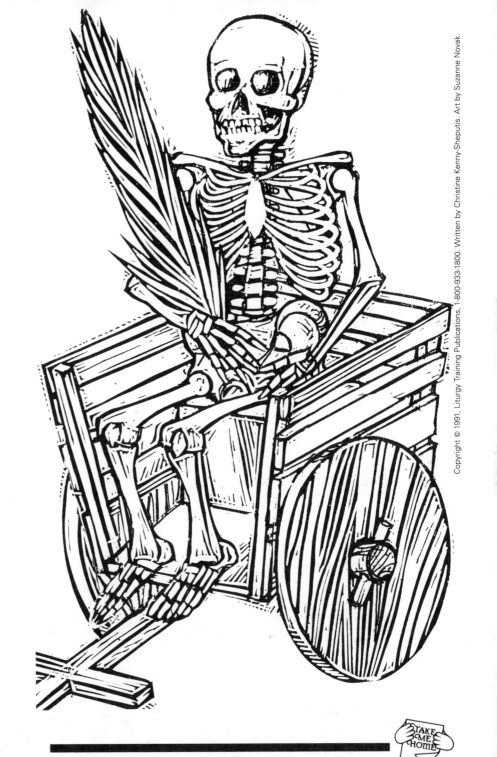

TAKE ME HOME

Memorial of St. Martin of Tours +397,
bishop
November 11

Martinmas

Snow and frost on St. Martin's Day, November 11, were once welcomed as Martin's own blessing. His feast day comes about the time of the year that winter announces itself. So Martin is sometimes pictured as a gruff "Old Man Winter," called "Furry Martin." Usually, though, Martin is pictured as a young, handsome soldier.

The story of St. Martin tells how, when he was a Roman centurion riding on a horse, he met a beggar on a snowy day. With nothing else to give, Martin cut his own cloak in half and shared it with the beggar. That night, in a dream, Christ appeared to Martin. Christ was wearing half of Martin's cloak!

When Martin became a Christian, he went through a lot of trouble to leave the army as a "conscientious objector." This is a person whose conscience tells him or her that it is wrong to fight in wars. Martin vowed that, because he was a Christian, it was not lawful for him to fight. From now on, he would only be a soldier for Christ.

An old custom calls for serving horseshoe-shaped cookies on St. Martin's Day. With an adult's help, make sugar cookie dough. Then roll it ¼ inch thick and cut it into strips ½ inch by 6 inches. On a cookie sheet, curve the strips into horseshoe shapes—like the letter U. Press sliced almonds into the dough. Bake 15 minutes at 325°.

Solemnity of Christ the King
The Sunday before Advent begins

Parish artisans can be helpful in a show-and-tell on how to make an Advent wreath. Of course, there are many other ways to count the days until Christmas, such as Advent calendars. What is key here is to build eagerness and anticipation—and not to jump the gun in celebration.

Advent has its own "look," distinct from Christmas. Parish meeting rooms and classrooms might show these distinctions— perhaps through the use of winter's colors (blues, purples, silvers) and decorations in Advent as distinct from Christmastime's familiar reds, whites, golds and greens.

Any groundwork in helping all parishioners to keep Advent as Advent must be done throughout the autumn; otherwise, if you wait until Advent itself when most folks' plans have been made, your efforts at education may be regarded as harsh interference.

Perhaps the take-home note for Advent (the first one in the book) can be brought home mid-November. Perhaps the Advent notes can be accompanied by the words of an Advent song to sing at home in prayer.

A Crown for King Jesus

Copyright © 1991, Liturgy Training Publications, 1-800-933-1800. Written by Christine Kenny-Sheputis. Art by Suzanne Novak.

Crowns and wreaths are common symbols of kingship. Some people have said that the circle of the seasons is Jesus' crown. Lord Jesus takes all of our years and sweeps them up into eternity. Jesus wears time like a crown!

Now is a good week to prepare an Advent wreath. To create a wreath that goes on the table, make a circle of evergreen branches and place it on a round tray or platter to catch candle drippings. Evenly space four candle holders around the ring.

To make a wreath that hangs from the ceiling, you will need an adult's help: Buy an already made evergreen wreath. Hang it horizontally over the table with four long, wide ribbons. (That's hard work, but the effect is wonderful.) For safety's sake, maybe the four candles can be placed on the table instead of on the wreath.

The old German custom uses four red candles. Some people use three purple candles for penance and one rose-colored candle for joy. You can use dark blue candles for waiting. Or use ordinary white candles, with purple and rose or blue ribbons.

On the Saturday night before the First Sunday of Advent, light one candle. Then light this one candle each night that week. Each Sunday until Christmas, light one more:

First one, then two,
Then three, then four,
And then the Christ Child
knocks on the door!

TAKE ME HOME

Thanksgiving Day
Second Monday in October in Canada
Fourth Thursday in November in the U.S.A.

We Gather Together

Most Thanksgiving foods—like turkey, pumpkins, cranberries, potatoes and corn—are foods of the Native North American peoples. Nowadays, just about everyone around the world eats these foods. Get ready for Thanksgiving by doing some research on the foods you eat. Where did they come from? Who grew or raised them? Who prepared them?

Besides God's gift of food, what other things are you thankful for? Thanksgiving Day was put on the calendar to thank God publicly for the opportunities and gifts that helped the English pilgrims survive—and thrive.

If you can, urge your household to thank God publicly at Mass or at a prayer service in your town. Most parishes have a special Thanksgiving liturgy.

Make up a Thanksgiving prayer to say before dinner with your guests or hosts. After dinner, before people have left the table, ask them what they are especially thankful for this year. You may need to start by talking about the people and things you are thankful for.

Be sure to sing songs this day. Almost everyone knows the tunes to a few songs of thanksgiving. Try "We gather together" or "Now thank we all our God." To help everyone join in, make copies of the words earlier in the week.

Sometimes, it is hard to say thanks the rest of the year. But Thanksgiving is *the* day for all of us to speak out.

TAKE ME HOME